PENLEE

The Loss of a Lifeboat

MICHAEL SAGAR-FENTON

First published in 1991 by Bossiney Books

This new and revised edition published by Truran

Truran is an imprint of Tor Mark Ltd,
United Downs Industrial Estate,
St Day, Redruth TR16 5HY

www.tormark.co.uk

Reprinted 2000, 2005, 2006, 2014
This edition 2021

ISBN 978 1 85022 260 6

Images: Andrew Besley; RNAS Culdrose; RNLI; Union Transport PLC; Del Johnson;
Nicholas Praed; thanks to Cornish Weekly Newspapers Ltd for the loan of photographs
from the Michael Williams Collection.

Map: Felicity Young

Printed and bound in the UK

FOREWORD

This book is a page-turner that can't be put down until it is done. It then stays with you for it demands contemplation. Most disasters are made up of a series of small but cumulative errors, decisions and circumstances until the moment of truth. Knowing the conclusion to this disaster makes it all the more poignant as you see the inevitable being swept along by a ferocious, cold and dispassionate storm.

During a project, 'Spirit of Mystery', to recreate a voyage made by seven Cornishmen from Newlyn to Melbourne for the Gold Rush in 1854 I met and got to know the 'Boys' of the Penlee Life Boat. We were moored up by the RNLI berth in Newlyn and were embraced by this warm and diverse group of people. The common theme being big hearts that are prepared to put others before themselves.

The night of 19 December 1981 wrought a storm of such malevolent power that only those made of greater stuff would stand up to it. The crew of the Penlee Lifeboat, and those they attempted to rescue, paid the ultimate price but there were others involved who gave their utmost. The helicopter crew leaps off the page with their bravery and skill.

If ever there was an example of the sea at its worst and humanity at its best then it is the story of the loss of the Penlee Lifeboat. This book will leave you feeling moved, proud and very humble as you reflect on what it must have been like for those brave men who gave their lives to a higher cause.

It is something to reflect on, even aspire too, certainly to support. So if you are browsing, then buy this book for in doing so you will be touched by something special and you will also be supporting the RNLI.

Pete Goss MBE

ABOUT THE AUTHOR

Michael Sagar-Fenton is a native of West Cornwall; born in Penzance in 1945 and educated in Penzance and Truro, he lives on the coast near Lamorna, close to the scene of much of this narrative. He is married with two children.

He is a regular contributor to a number of newspapers and magazines, in particular The Cornishman and is the author of other books on local themes.

He began gathering material for this book soon after the incident in 1981, but respecting the wishes of the relatives, it was not published until 1991. It received a warm response from sources as diverse as John Le Carré who named it as his 'Book of the Year' to one of the relatives who wrote to thank him for "bringing the boys back".

This is a reprint of the enlarged and revised edition.

Wherever possible the book is based on first-hand interviews and other original unpublished material.

ACKNOWLEDGEMENTS

I would like to thank all those who consented to be interviewed for this book, in particular those who did so against their better judgement, after unhappy experiences with the press and media. I thank them for their trust and I hope I have earned it.

Thanks for their help and hospitality to: RNAS Culdrose; HM Coastguard Falmouth; RNLI Poole; Department of Transport Maritime Museum, Holborn; Harry Rayner; RNLI Penlee - especially John Corin; to my wife for her encouragement over ten years; to Peter Wright-Davies; to Lindsey Innis; to Michael Williams; and to all others who have given their time and assistance. My particular gratitude finally to the late Peter Garnier, former Chairman of Penlee Branch, without whose encouragement this book might never have materialised.

Thanks are due to Pete Goss for writing the foreword to this edition.

THE PEOPLE

UNION STAR

Master	Henry 'Mick' Moreton
Mate	James Whittaker
Engineer	George Sedgwick
Crew	Agostinho Verressimo
Crew	Manuel Lopez

MASTER'S FAMILY

Wife	Dawn Moreton
Stepdaughter	Sharon Brown
Stepdaughter	Deanne Brown

PENLEE RNLI CREW

Coxswain	Trevelyan Richards
2nd Cox/Mechanic	Stephen Madron
2nd Mechanic	Nigel Brockman
Crew	John Blewett
Crew	Charles Greenhaugh
Crew	Kevin Smith
Crew	Barrie Torrie
Crew	Gary Wallis

OFFICERS

Honorary Secretary	Del Johnson
Deputy Launching Authority	Clive Bennett
Deputy Launching Authority	Michael Sutherland
Head Launcher	Dudley Penrose

SENNEN RNLI

Coxswain	Maurice Hutchens

LIZARD/CADGWITH RNLI
Coxswain   Peter Mitchell

ST MARY'S RNLI
Coxswain   Matt Lethbridge

HM COASTGUARDS
District Controller   Siriol 'Robbie' Roberts
Watch Officer   Colin Sturman
Watch Officer   Sidney Winchcombe
Sector Officer   Donald Buckfield

MOUSEHOLE COASTAL RESCUE COMPANY
Mike Buttery
Douglas Hoare
Richard Hoare
Harry Pender

RNAS SEA KING R80
Captain   Russell Smith
Co-pilot   Ken Docherty
Observer   Martin Kennie
Winchman   Steven Marlow

UNION TRANSPORT
Assistant Ships Superintendent Malcolm Fisher
Fleet Operations Director Harry Rayner

WEISSMULLER - TUG NOORD HOLLAND
Master   Guy Buurman
Headquarters   M Van Der Merwe

TO THE EIGHT AND THE OTHER EIGHT

FALMOUTH MARITIME RESCUE CENTRE IN 1981, WHICH WAS OFFICIALLY OPENED ONLY THREE WEEKS BEFORE THE PENLEE DISASTER. DISTRICT CONTROLLER 'ROBBIE' ROBERTS ON LEFT.

ONE

DECEMBER 19, 1981
18.04

Union Star to Land's End Radio: Calling - this is Union Star calling Land's End Coastguard.
Falmouth Coastguard: Receiving.
Union Star: Yes, I am approximately eight miles east of Wolf Rock. My engines have stopped, unable to start at the moment. Could you please have a helicopter standing by for us?
Falmouth Coastguard: Your position eight miles east of Wolf Rock. Is that correct?
Union Star: Yes that is correct and there are eight people aboard - eight people aboard.
Falmouth Coastguard: What type of vessel are you, Union Star?
Union Star: We are a coaster - 1400 dead weight.
Falmouth Coastguard: 1400 dead weight. What cargo please?
Union Star: Cargo is fertiliser and it is in piles.
Falmouth Coastguard: Roger. Yes. What are your intentions? Are you going to anchor?
Union Star: Our intentions are at the moment we want to get the main engines started. If we cannot get the main engines started we will have to take everybody off and get someone to tow us in.
Falmouth Coastguard: Roger. Stand by this channel. Just to confirm, you are eight miles east of Wolf Rock.
Union Star: Yes that is correct.
Falmouth Coastguard: Roger. Thank you. Stand by Channel 16.
Union Star: Thank you. Standing by.

Five hours earlier on the 19th December, 1981 the Crescent Line coaster Eminence, steaming up the English Channel, hailed a trim brand-new coaster heading the other way. They were just south of the Eddystone Light, and although the water was choppy with the beginnings of a running sea, the other vessel was making light work of it. After a brief chat, the Eminence continued eastwards, with the wind in her favour. The other vessel, the Union Star, also continued on course, heading into the weather.

Although she was going well, the Union Star's captain, Henry 'Mick' Moreton, had an awkward decision to face. Ever since 05.30 that morning the weather forecast had included a warning for the Plymouth area, indicating a short-lived but possibly intense gale from the south. At lunchtime, soon after he had greeted the Eminence, worse news arrived over Moreton's radio: "Plymouth, southerly 5 increasing gale 8 to storm 10, moderating 6 to gale 8 later. Rain. Good visibility becoming moderate".

It was the first mention of a storm force 10.

The Union Star was on passage from the Dutch port of IJmuiden to Arklow, a port on the east coast of the Irish Republic just to the south of Wicklow. Her cargo - her first - was 1250 tonnes of calcium ammonium nitrate in bulk, or ordinary agricultural fertiliser compound. It was a straightforward and routine passage for a coaster - across the North Sea, through the Strait of Dover, then hugging the south coast of England until the corner of Land's End was turned, and a straight run up the Irish Sea to her destination. Four days were allowed for the voyage, which had begun at 17.00 on the 17th.

Moreton's choice was either to keep going or to make for shelter. The gale was due from the south, which meant that if he could get to Land's End he could then run before the storm up the Irish Sea, or if necessary slip into the shelter of St Ives Bay until it moderated. However, the southerly set of the wind effectively ruled out the other usual alternative, which was to steam into the corner of Mount's Bay and take shelter off Newlyn. The only safe anchorage on the south coast of Cornwall would be in Falmouth Roads. This was a considerable detour - about two hours' steaming each way, plus whatever time he had to wait.

Normally this would not have been of much consequence. The four days allowed a fair margin of time to cope with unforeseeable weather conditions, and they were in any case scheduled to arrive on a Sunday, which was not a working day in the port of Arklow. However, Moreton was already behind schedule.

Henry Moreton was something of a rising star in the world of coastal shipping. Thirty-two years old, he had obtained his Master's ticket at the young age of twenty-seven and was making a name for himself as a hard-working and energetic young man, destined to go far. Since joining Union Transport, the company which owned the *Union Star*, he had been put in charge of two of their older vessels, and he had made such dramatic improvements in their morale and efficiency that he had been rewarded with the new *Union Star* over the heads of older and more experienced captains. Such men are often respected more than they are liked, but Moreton seems to have impressed everyone with his good nature as well as his skill, and was popular with his crews. He was tall and slightly piratical in appearance, with bright eyes and long dark hair tied back in a pony-tail. He was calm, competent and resourceful. He was also ambitious and self-confident, on the crest of a wave.

He had made his home near Harwich where he lived with his South African-born wife Dawn. Dawn was blonde and petite, less flamboyant than her husband, and when she could not travel with him - she sometimes signed on for a voyage as cook - she lived the quiet lonely life of a sea-captain's wife. They had no children of their own, but Dawn had two young teenage daughters by a previous marriage, Sharon and Deanne, who lived in South Africa with her ex-husband but came over on visits when possible.

In December 1981 the children had come over for the Christmas holiday. Moreton's offer of a trip on the *Union Star* was too good to refuse, but it also meant that he would be at sea most of the time the girls were staying, and would not even be home for Christmas. It may have been possible to have obtained permission for them all to sail with him, but it was not a simple matter. It was not at the discretion of Union Transport themselves, but with the owners of the cargo, and there may have been extra insurance implications. In any case, Moreton declined to go through the whole complicated process.

Instead, when he left IJmuiden on Thursday evening's tide, he had turned not south-west for the Dover Strait, but had headed almost due west, cutting across the North Sea. By 8.30 next morning, he was anchored off the port of Brightlingsea, near Colchester. He paused for only a matter of minutes while a launch brought Dawn, Sharon and Deanne out to meet him, and as soon as they were safely aboard he proceeded at full speed on his resumed journey.

Friday had been an idyllic day, calm and sunny. Most of the crew were young, and the *Union Star* was clean and new, undemanding of much attention. The presence of Dawn and the two lively girls was a welcome diversion for them all. They steamed down the Channel, so relaxed that Moreton forgot even to make his daily call-in to the office until 19.30 in the evening.

Saturday was different from the start, dull, cold and windy. During the day conditions grew more unpleasant. And now a storm was awaiting them.

Moreton was a seaman above all. He had been at sea from a young age, and was no stranger to bad weather. He liked the class of vessel he was on and had been through many a gale on his previous command the *Union Jupiter*. There was deep water ahead and little prospect of actual danger provided that he kept a generous distance between himself and the shore. The next few hours promised to be uncomfortable at the least, especially for the family. However, he had lost seven or eight hours in collecting them. If it later seemed that he had lost further time taking shelter merely to protect them - supposing that Union Transport came to know of their presence at all - he might not look such a professional, not quite so dedicated to his company. Moreton weighed all this up in a moment.

He elected to keep going.

———————————

NO PHOTOGRAPHS EXIST OF *UNION STAR* WHICH PERISHED ON HER MAIDEN VOYAGE. THIS IS *UNION MARS* WHICH WAS IDENTICAL IN DESIGN.

The wind rose in earnest as the afternoon went on. It began to drag waves up from the south, big waves, which were soon breaking over the coaster's side decks. She began to roll in the sharp, stiff movement which was typical of her design. She rounded the Lizard and started to beat across Mount's Bay at reduced speed. The wind direction could hardly have been less favourable. Most gales in Mount's Bay roar up from the south-west, so that down-Channel traffic can at least parry the waves on the port bow, and leave a last haven of shelter if needed. This time the whole bay was exposed and unsafe, and the waves beat mercilessly full on the port beam of the Union Star. Heavy seas began to loom over her, breaking across her hatches and driving her further and further over into the troughs. Her roll increased to wicked proportions and the wind began to fleck the sea with foam.

For the family the pleasure cruise was turning into a feat of endurance. But if Moreton regretted his decision to continue on their behalf, he had no qualms at all about his ship.

The Union Star was a shallow-draught low air-profile coaster, purpose-built for what is known as the 'near-Continental' trade, moving goods about in the increasingly busy EU trading area. She was designed to operate not only in coastal waters but also in the great navigable rivers of Europe, thus eliminating the need to transfer goods from sea-going vessels to river barges Such was the demand for the services of this kind of vessel that no fewer than four were ordered and built for Union Transport in 1981 at a cost of over a million pounds apiece. She had been built by Nordsøvaerflet NS of Ringkøping, Denmark, and her vital statistics were 67.6 metres (222ft) long, 11.2 metres (37ft) beam, 935 gross tonnage, and a draught of about 3.2 metres (10.5ft). She had passed her trials without a hitch, except for grounding on a mud bank for a short while outside the port of Esbjerg.

Like her sister ships she was registered not in the United Kingdom but in Dublin, Republic of Ireland. The Republic of Ireland is not a 'flag of convenience' - a country with less stringent regulations regarding manning levels, safety, certification and other expensive considerations. The main reason given by Union Transport for registering its fleet there was that British regulations at the time forbade the use of foreign nationals as masters of British ships. Several of Union Transport's masters were in fact German - valued for their knowledge of the inland waterways - and Union Transport preferred to keep them on. The Union Star was certificated for use in the North Sea, the Channel, the Irish Sea and Irish coastal waters, provided that her distance from the coast or nearest port did not exceed 200 nautical miles.

There were four other crew members aboard the coaster, as she forged on into the gloomy afternoon.

James Whittaker was the mate, only 26 and similar to Moreton in his competence and ambition. Young and good humoured, he had just married.

George Sedgwick, the engineer, was 50 years old with a lifetime's experience of the sea. Regulations requiring a specific engineer for ships of this size had only just come into force and so Sedgwick had joined the Union Star just before her departure. To ensure that he was familiar with the engine room layout and procedure he had already been to Arklow the previous week on a sister ship, the Union Venus, and to be doubly sure Union Transport's Ships' Superintendent had spent a few hours with him in the Union Star's engine room just before she set forth.

Two ordinary seamen made up the crew, Agostinho Verressimo aged 24, and Manuel Jesus Lopez, 21, both originally from the Portuguese Cape Verde Islands. Like many of their countrymen they had come to spend a few years as seamen in Europe before returning home, hopefully with their savings. They had been personally chosen by Moreton who had sailed with them both before. Both had good references, and were reluctantly yielded up by their present captains. Both spoke English - Verressimo better than Lopez - and were competent and popular.

Under British Regulations, a ship of the *Union Star's* size should have carried a second mate. However she was on the margin even for the British rules, and the Irish Regulations did not require it. Also, for a UK Safe Deck Manning Certificate, three rather than two seamen would probably have been required, but again these regulations allowed for a good deal of time spent on maintenance. Being brand new, *Union Star* had little need of maintenance on her maiden voyage, and so the five men who put to sea on 17th December seemed sufficient to sail the routine passage to Arklow without difficulty.

During the afternoon Moreton was listening, as most seamen do, to Channel 16, the open two-way radio channel. By coincidence he discovered that his previous command the *Union Jupiter* was just across the other side of the narrow peninsula, taking shelter in St Ives Bay. He had a long and happy conversation with her new captain, Ian Cooke, unable to resist making unfavourable comparisons between the way the *Jupiter* would have coped with the weather conditions and the way the *Star* was coping. Professionally he was delighted with her handling, even glad to see her put to the test. His confidence in her was absolute.

But he was wrong.

Even as he spoke the seeds of the *Union Star's* destruction were being sown. Just below where he stood, unknown to the captain, the integrity of the ship had already been breached, and mortal damage was occurring.

Where the side deck joined the vertical rear superstructure on the port side were three protruding pipes, which let into the fuel tanks. One was the filler pipe, and next to it the smaller sounding pipe for checking the fuel level, both covered by brass screw caps with a retaining chain. The third was the ventilator, capped by the blue cowl of a 'Pres-Vac' valve. The valve was merely a sophisticated version of a diver's snorkel, i.e. it remained open unless water entered it, in which case a hollow float would rise up and block the aperture. It is a well-proven and widely used device, which has been known to admit a small leak of water on occasions, but never such quantities as would be needed to trouble the powerful and hardy Alpha diesel engine of the *Union Star*.

Although she had reduced speed, the *Union Star* was still travelling at 6-8 knots. Every few moments green seas came across her side decks, swirling fiercely where they met the wall of the rear section, where the three pipes stood.

It is a remote possibility that an undamaged valve could have sprung a sudden leak, or that a piece of flotsam struck it, but the likelihood is that, for one reason or another, one of the screw caps on one of the other pipes was not tightly closed. The boat's vibration or the turbulence of the water could then have unscrewed it altogether, leaving the pipe open and unprotected. Seawater could then have flowed freely in large quantities down the pipe and into the fuel tank with every wave, as it surely did.

Moreton was wholly ignorant of his peril. The worst part of the voyage was almost over as the dull afternoon turned to evening. He was taking a beeline across Mount's Bay, bearing due east of the Wolf Rock lighthouse to keep him well off the rocks by Land's End. In less than an hour he could gratefully turn the *Union Star's* bows to the north and her stern to the increasingly fierce weather. The ship passed well to the south of Penzance, Newlyn and Mousehole, her lights invisible in the squalls and drizzle.

IN 1981, THE ROYAL NAVAL AIR STATION AT CULDROSE, WAS ON CALL FOR RESCUE WORK. THIS OFTEN INVOLVED WORKING IN APPALLING CONDITIONS AT SEA OR HOVERING ABOVE CLIFFS. IN THE IMAGE A SEA KING PRACTICES PICKING UP SURVIVORS FROM A LIFE RAFT.

Towards the end of the afternoon watch it was customary for the engineer on duty to pump up fuel from the main storage tanks to the daily service tank, which held 8,800 litres, sufficient fuel for a day's operation, and fed directly into the main engine.

The coaster was still performing splendidly if increasingly uncomfortably, forging along the crests and troughs, embattled but well ballasted by the full load of fertiliser and in no appreciable danger.

Then the steady subconscious heartbeat of the engine suddenly coughed. It became irregular - stopped - started - and cut out altogether, leaving a frightening silence, filled only by the whistling of the wind and the crashing of the waves.

The engine powered the dynamo for all the main electric circuits, and so when it stopped so also did the lights, the heaters, and the radar. The 24-volt emergency battery came on, which supplied only the compass, radio/telephone and some emergency lighting.

The *Union Star* continued for a while under her own momentum, slowing gradually to a stop. Her position relative to the sea remained the same, the natural position of a drifting vessel, broadside to the waves. As helpless as any sailing ship of old, she began to drive northward before the wind and waves towards the granite bones of West Penwith.

TWO

———————

The waters of Mount's Bay are unfortunately no strangers to such a scene. It is probably the earliest recorded trading port in Britain, a safe haven and good anchorage in most weathers. However, at a trick of the wind, its embrace can change into a deadly maritime trap. Over the centuries, hundreds of good vessels have found the fierce Atlantic gales pressing them towards the coast, with the Lizard unreachably far in one direction and Land's End similarly too far in the other. There was no escape, and their best hope was to be wrecked on the sands and not on the reefs and shoals, or against the cliffs.

Despite the persistent legends of wrecking, history records that the response of those who lived around the bay to a vessel in trouble was courageous and humane. Fishermen would go out at real risk to their own lives to pluck survivors from wrecks, often under the frightened eyes of their families, and would not give up while there was anyone alive to save. Having done this, they would happily set to at the earliest possible opportunity and pick the wreck clean.

When the *National Institution for the Preservation of Life from Shipwreck* was formed in 1824 - later to become the RNLI - it merely gave form to a long tradition of bravery and service. Lifeboat stations were established at Penzance, Sennen, St Ives, The Lizard and the Isles of Scilly, and for a while at Porthleven, Mullion and Hayle, and carried on the tradition under the RNLI banner, saving many hundreds of lives, often in extreme circumstances.

It was not until the 1960s that their role as frontline rescuers began to be supported. The Royal Naval Air Station at Culdrose, near Porthleven, gradually became almost exclusively a helicopter base, and a skilful Air-Sea Rescue team was set up. This provided useful real-life training for the Navy, which had huge advantages in speed and access to dangerous positions. But whenever the wind rose to gale force, helicopter crewmen and lifeboatmen alike would be on the alert, ready to run at a moment's notice and face whatever hazards awaited them.

———————

An engine breakdown, though always deeply disconcerting, is far from an unheard of event, and Moreton had had his share. He was equally at home in the engine room as Sedgwick, so between them by the dim light of the emergency bulkhead lighting, they searched for obvious symptoms.

There were none. The pipes and valves, still new, gleamed back at them, unblemished. The gauges showed plenty of fuel, with no air bubbles. The temperature gauges were normal. There were no splits or leaks. It might have been a temporary blockage, some careless finishing of the new engine, a major defect which had just come to light, or just a temporary hiccough. Moreton had no way of telling.

In the hope that it was something simple, Moreton tried time and again to restart the engine, the sound of the starter echoing through the ship. The starter was turned by compressed air, stored in two metal flasks. Soon it began to run out and the starter ran slower and slower until all power was gone. The compressed air could only be replenished by running either the main engines or one of the auxiliary generators for at least ten minutes. They could not coax any life into them either.

It was a bitter moment. Moreton was naturally self-reliant and did not like to ask for help. He also did not particularly wish to draw attention to himself and his passengers. However, as an experienced and pragmatic seaman he had to face the facts, and they were that his ship was without power, driving towards a notorious lee shore in a gathering storm. They would probably be able to correct their mysterious fault. On the other hand they might not. There was only one proper course to take, and Moreton - however reluctant - did not try to evade it.

It was 18.04. Moreton picked up his radio.

The first calm exchange between the Union Star and Falmouth Coastguard masked troubled situations on both sides of the call.

Despite the conditions, Moreton did not really consider that the Union Star was in any immediate danger. He had given a wide berth to the toe of the Land's End peninsula, about 9.6km (six miles) by his own reckoning, which should give them sufficient time to sort the engine out. He was not one to run away at the first signs of trouble and nor were his crew. But Dawn, Deanne and Sharon complicated the picture. He had invited them along for pleasure not danger. If there was going to be trouble, he wanted them out of the way, for their sakes and his own. Conditions on board, wallowing in heavy seas without light or heating, were already highly unpleasant. If they could not fix the engine fairly quickly he would call for a helicopter - RNAS Culdrose was only a few miles across the bay - and have the women taken off. As for the rest, they would stay until they absolutely had to leave.

Falmouth Maritime Rescue Co-ordination Centre was a newly formed regional nerve-centre. In recent years the Coastguard Service had been undergoing a radical and painful change, with the emphasis on reducing the number of coastguards and auxiliaries, closing down several smaller coastguard stations, and largely abandoning visual watches. Instead resources had been concentrated into high-technology super-stations, on the rationale that most distress situations were reported and dealt with by radio and that most visual watches were a waste of time and money. This had caused considerable controversy with passions roused on both sides - those in favour describing the critics as being old-fashioned and impractical, and those against describing it as a cynical exercise in cost cutting which would lead to increased danger and loss of life. The Falmouth Centre had only just been established and the argument was at its height. Land's End Coastguard Station - to whom Union Star's first call was addressed - was one of the victims of the new order and was no longer manned on a full-time basis. It was however, still operating as a radio and radar station in bad weather.

Moreton's call was taken by Colin Sturman, the senior watch officer on duty. As an experienced naval officer and coastguard it did not take him a moment to appreciate that, although not in imminent peril, the Union Star's position was potentially very sticky indeed. However, it was up to the captain to decide what level of assistance was needed, not the coastguards. Moreton sounded calm and competent, and Sturman was content to let him make the pace. Problems like the Union Star's were not exceptional, and the probable outcome was that she would sort out her engine trouble or at least make some kind of temporary fix, and steam away for shelter. There was no point in Sturman initiating an all-out rescue operation under those circumstances. In coastguard terms, it was an 'Alert' phase, and the procedure was to inform the various rescue services without calling any of them into action.

The news of the coaster's troubles began to spread. Sturman ordered Officer Winchcombe to request a Sea King helicopter to be brought to readiness. He ordered Officer Notley to request the Penlee lifeboat to "anticipate". He himself contacted the Land's End station at Gwennap Head to investigate the possibility of arranging a tow. He knew that an ocean-going tug was usually on permanent station in Mount's Bay, ready to steam at short notice to any situation which might require its services. Land's End confirmed that such a tug was on station, the Noord Holland, owned by Weissmuller of Ijmuiden, Captain Guy Buurman. Sturman called up Buurman at once.

Guy Buurman was a mature and highly experienced Dutch sea-captain, a larger-than-life character, well-known around the coasts of Europe. On the night of the 19th, he had his own problems, in the shape of a defective radar set which required him to return to Falmouth the following day, and an increasingly exposed

COLIN STURMAN OF THE COASTGUARD SERVICE, SENIOR WATCH OFFICER ON THE NIGHT OF 19 DECEMBER 1981.

and uncomfortable anchorage, off Penlee Quarry in the normally peaceful area known as Gwavas Lake. By established habit the open Channel - Channel 16 - was on continuous broadcast throughout the tug's accommodation, and Buurman's sharp ears had already picked up the Union Star's call and gauged its significance. He was anticipating the call from Falmouth when it came.

Sturman greeted him, repeated the information he had to hand and asked if the Noord Holland was willing and able to assist. Buurman assessed the situation. Under international maritime law all vessels in the vicinity are required to respond to a Mayday, the international distress call. However, the Union Star did not appear to be in actual distress and had issued no Mayday, so Buurman was quite free to refuse. On the other hand, the Union Star was a potential piece of business for a salvage tug. It was for such reasons that Weissmuller kept him in Mount's Bay. He decided to offer the Union Star Lloyds Open Form. This is an internationally recognised open contract by which a vessel agrees to accept a tow and to pay an appropriate sum to be determined later for the service. It was the only agreement which Buurman was empowered to make without further reference to his head office.

It involved an element of risk on both sides. If the tug was unable to assist the rule was 'No cure - no pay'. However if it succeeded in getting a line aboard and effecting a tow, Union Transport would be liable for a hefty charge, even if the ship's problem later turned out to be trivial.

He told Sturman that he would proceed if the Union Star would agree to Lloyds Open Form, and Sturman advised him to call the Union Star directly and sort out the arrangements between them.

18.10

Falmouth Coastguard to Union Star: I have a salvage tug and he is available if required. Would you like him to come and stand by you?
Union Star: Yes if possible please.
Falmouth Coastguard: The salvage tug is the Noord Holland. He will probably call you on Channel 16 shortly.
Union Star: OK, thank you very much, we are just drifting towards the land very slowly at the moment. We are trying to start the engine. If we get it under way and get clear we will let you know later.

A couple of minutes later the Noord Holland did indeed call the Union Star. They changed to a working Channel, Channel 9, to discuss the situation further.

In the meantime, Winchcombe, in accordance with procedure, had contacted Plymouth Search & Rescue Co-ordination Centre with a situation report, and they had passed on the request for a Sea King to stand by.

COASTGUARD OFFICER WINCHCOMBE WHO CALLED FOR THE HELICOPTER CREW TO STAND BY.

Notley was having a more difficult time trying to contact the Penlee lifeboat. He telephoned the Honorary Secretary, Del Johnson, who was the person primarily responsible for decisions to launch. Mrs Johnson answered to say that Del was out for the evening and referred him to the Deputy Launching Authority, Clive Bennett. Notley got no reply at all from this number, and turned to the next number on his list, Captain Mike Sutherland, the second DLA. Mrs Sutherland was at home at the time, but for some reason her telephone did not ring. Notley, frustrated, turned to the next authority for Penlee, and rang the coxswain Trevelyan Richards himself. At last he found himself talking to an authorised representative of the Lifeboat Station. He gave him the news of the Union Star's breakdown and the contact with the Noord Holland. He asked the lifeboat to stand by. According to Notley, he asked the lifeboat to "anticipate" and the crew to "muster in the boathouse", and he finished the call with the clear impression that the lifeboat would be brought to a situation of immediate readiness, with the men in the boathouse, ready to jump aboard and launch at a moment's notice.

However, whether or not Notley made himself clear, that is not the way things were done at Penlee. The boathouse was cold, cramped and inhospitable, without even the most basic facilities. If the men had to wait there for long periods every time there was an incident they would be frozen stiff before they even started. The boathouse was less than half a mile from the village and so it was customary for the crew, having been contacted by telephone, to wait at home for the signal. That is what happened on this occasion. Richards rang Stephen Madron, first mechanic, and Nigel Brockman, second mechanic. Mrs Madron said that Stephen was in Newlyn and she would contact him at once. Nigel Brockman was at home, and offered to pass the word on. Mary Richards, Trevelyan's mother, suggested pragmatically that if he might be called out later it would be as well if he had his tea straight away, and started to lay the table.

Meanwhile, on Channel 9, Buurman and Moreton were having a disagreement. Buurman found Moreton calm and controlled at first, but when he started to discuss terms, the tone of the conversation changed. Moreton wanted him to merely come and stand by, to be on hand if they were unable to re-start the engines. Buurman pointed out that there was no official distress situation, and that he could not weigh anchor and proceed without the authority of his owners, except under Lloyds Open Form. His owners would probably then have to contact the Union Star's owners - and so on and so on.

Moreton had his own protocols to worry about. His Master's Manual was quite clear on the procedures. If he required assistance:

"1) Not to hesitate to call for help if you think it reasonably necessary for the safety of the ship and cargo.

2) Not to refuse an offer of aid made with a claim for salvage in mind unless you are reasonably certain that other assistance on ordinary contractual terms can be obtained in good time.

3) In the last resort to act without higher instructions if necessary to engage salvage assistance."

However, this was in the rule book. In practice, if he agreed to an open salvage contract costing thousands of pounds and it turned out to be a simple repair job, he could look forward at least to considerable loss of face, and probably the displeasure of his employers with its subsequent effect on his career. Time seemed to be on his side, and it was simply too soon to commit himself to a salvage deal. If Buurman was unwilling to stand by, then he, Moreton, had better things to do than to argue with him.

Buurman found Moreton "short-tempered", and assumed that the situation on the Union Star was not as serious as it had seemed. However, his instinct told him that in these conditions any breakdown was serious. After a short period of reflection, he put through a call to Weissmuller in Ijmuiden.

OPPOSITE: THE OCEAN-GOING TUG NOORD HOLLAND, WHICH WENT TO THE AID OF THE UNION STAR.

18.16

<u>Falmouth Coastguard to Union Star:</u> Have you had a word with the salvage tug skipper?
<u>Union Star:</u> Yes. All he is interested in is the money at the moment. We are holding steady as we are. We don't seem to be drifting into land.

Moreton could never have conceived the devastating effect these few testy words would have on his reputation. After a pause he decided to reveal his main concern.

<u>Union Star:</u> All we request. we have one woman, two children and the crew. If possible just a helicopter standing by to take them off.

18. 17

<u>Falmouth Coastguard:</u> Yes we have Penlee Lifeboat anticipatory, she is just to the north of you, just this side of Newlyn, and there is a Sea King helicopter being made ready at Culdrose. Could you give me the ages of the children please?
<u>Union Star:</u> 14 and 15 years of age.
Falmouth Coastguard: Roger, 14 and 15 years of age, one woman and five of the crew, over.
<u>Union Star:</u> Yes that is correct.
<u>Falmouth Coastguard:</u> You are in no difficulty at the moment, just trying to get the engine started but holding your position. Is that correct. over?
<u>Union Star:</u> Yes that is correct. Just at the present moment of time - touch wood - we are not in any major difficulty.

Buurman contacted a Mr Van der Merwe at Weissmuller headquarters. On being informed of Moreton's reaction, Van der Merwe's attitude was that Buurman was perfectly justified in staying put for the time being. He offered to contact the Union Star's headquarters and continue negotiations on an office-to-office basis. However, Buurman had been thinking it over. Mount's Bay was becoming rapidly untenable as an anchorage, and although it was against his wishes to leave when he had a scheduled trip to Falmouth the next day, Buurman had well-honed survival instincts. His experience told him to make preparations to leave before he was forced to. The fact that this also coincided with the Union Star's wishes was a factor, but his main concern was for the safety of his own vessel. This he felt could best be ensured by being at sea and under way rather than waiting for trouble to come to him. Weighing anchor in that position could be a long and tedious process in his experience, due to the number of discarded fishing ropes and trawl wires which tended to come up with the chain and had to be cut away.

He put it to Van der Merwe that all things considered he would rather get under way without further delay and proceed directly towards the coaster's reported position. Van der Merwe deferred without question to his captain's decision. A few minutes later - and only about fifteen minutes after the first report of the breakdown - Buurman commenced the process of weighing anchor and getting under way. For the moment he told no one but his owners of his intentions.

At Falmouth, after the first flurry of action, there was time to reflect. All the coastguard officers were experienced mariners. No one liked the 'feel' of the situation. Winchcombe noted that although the situation was far from critical there was a strong sense of foreboding. Sturman agreed. He decided that a call to the district controller was in order and rang him at home. District Controller Roberts' reaction to the situation was instantly to set off for the control centre. Sturman passed a situation report to Plymouth, who confirmed that a helicopter was being brought to readiness. Continuing to use his head, Sturman decided to try to get a more accurate fix on where the Union Star actually was. Eight miles east of the Wolf Rock put her about six-seven miles south of the shore, but in that weather each mile would be crucial and it would be best to be sure. Don Buckfield was the coastguard sector officer for the Penzance area, the local man who attended calls and dealt with matters on the spot. He lived in a coastguard cottage about 91 metres (100 yds) from Land's End Coastguard Station, and at about 18.27 Sturman called him up, told him what was going on, and asked him to go up to the station and run a radar search. From that headland position he should be able to pick up the Union Star fairly accurately. Buckfield agreed, and set out through the atrocious night to the station.

Five minutes passed, and then the tension was broken by a message from the Union Star whose tone was as calm as its message was plaintive.

18.33
Union Star to Falmouth Coastguard: Could you give me the latest on the weather please?
Falmouth Coastguard: Yes, Land's End tells us the wind is just west of south, Force 8 gusting to 10 or 11. The latest shipping forecast for sea area Plymouth at 17.50 is "Southerly gale 8 to storm 10, decreasing 6 later. Rain at times, poor becoming good". Over.
Union Star: Thank you very much Falmouth. It's all understood. Thank you very much.

While the Union Star was left to ponder on the word "later", Falmouth tried to find out more.

Falmouth Coastguard: Any news on your engines yet?
Union Star: No not yet, we are still working on it. We'll let you know later on whether we get a yes or no on it.
Falmouth Coastguard: Roger. Have you had any communication from your owner reference the tow, over?

This appeared to be a completely novel idea to the Union Star. The mate was at the radio and asked Falmouth in the most polite terms if they would mind informing Union Transport of what was taking place. He said they "hadn't had time" to do it themselves. Sturman, willing to do anything to help, agreed. He tried Union Transport's offices. There was no answer. Captain Cooke on the Union Jupiter in St Ives Bay - one of a growing army of silent radio witnesses called in to help, giving the telephone numbers of the duty officers at Union Transport. Like so many others on the Saturday night before Christmas, one or two of them were out. Sturman finally got through at 18.46 to Assistant Ships' Superintendent Fisher, and explained to him the peril his company's newest vessel was in.

Meanwhile District Controller Roberts arrived at Falmouth and almost as he did so Don Buckfield called in his first findings from the radar screen at Land's End. The radar was set far from new and took some time to warm up, and in the computer and satellite age of Falmouth it may have seemed a somewhat old-fashioned tool.

COASTGUARD SECTOR OFFICER
DON BUCKFIELD.

Buckfield had three echoes on his screen, three blips of light in his scan of the increasingly fierce waters of the bay. He took Moreton's reported breakdown position as his central point and plotted the three echoes in relation to it. One he called 'Echo C' was a long way to the south-east. One which he called 'Echo B' was about 5.6km (3.5 miles) to the south-east of the breakdown position.

The one which caught his eye, 'Echo A', was almost due north of the position, down wind where one might expect the Union Star to be. But it was the relative distance that particularly struck him. It was 3.6km (2.25 miles) nearer to the coast from where Moreton thought he had broken down. There were only two explanations either the Union Star had been closer to shore when her engines suddenly failed her, or she was drifting far faster than anyone thought. After ten minutes Buckfield called in again. Echoes 'B' and 'C' were remaining more or less stable. 'Echo A' had moved northwards.

By 19.00 that evening the Union Star was at the centre of a web of anxious activity.

At Culdrose on the eastern side of the bay, the bleepers had summoned the four emergency helicopter crewmen from their houses. They had convened and were being briefed while the helicopter was made ready. As yet they had no orders to fly, but already the wind conditions were deteriorating, promising a 'hairy' mission.

Over in Mousehole Trevelyan Richards and Nigel Brockman, who had called round for news, were finishing tea. Trevelyan had got his charts out and was studying them. He knew that part of the coast as well as anyone alive, having set crab-pots out there since he was a boy. Still he wished to remind himself of the rocks and shoals once again the shoreline is a very different place in a raging storm at night. There are mischievous rocks which emerge only from time to time, at certain states of tide and sea. Then they rise suddenly from a trough, in the words of a local fisherman, "Tall as a house, water pouring off them, roaring like a lion". Richards studied sombrely.

Less than a mile away from where they sat, the Noord Holland had got under way at last, unbeknown to everyone. As Buurman turned her south-westwards and began to come out of Mount's Bay, he encountered sea conditions which exceeded his worst expectations. The waves were short and very steep with big breaking crests, up to 4.5-6 metres (15-20ft) high. Buurman had spent a lifetime at sea and was not easily impressed, but he later described these waves as having a quality "...which for the combination of size and steepness was the worst I have ever seen." He throttled back his two powerful engines and ploughed into the frightening seas at a respectful 4 -5 knots.

At Falmouth, District Controller Roberts had taken over command of the operation. He, like Sturman, liked the situation less and less as it went on. Just before the hour he received two reports which added to his anxieties. The first was a standard warning from Plymouth that icing conditions might prevent helicopter operations after 20.30. The other was the third set of radar fixes from Buckfield at Land's End. Once again Echoes 'B' and 'C' had not moved in a significant way. 'Echo A' was now 4.8km (three miles) north of Moreton's first position, drifting at a steady 1.5 knots. Buckfield's fix showed her to be only 5.5km (3.5 miles) from the rocks.

In Kent, Mr Fisher of Union Transport had received a call from Weissmuller in Holland, stating their readiness to assist and offering Lloyds Open Form. Fisher, who had been trying to contact his own superiors, was in a difficult position. He had so far been unable to raise the Union Star himself and had no idea how extreme Moreton's situation was. Until he knew his captain's assessment of the situation he was unwilling to go over his head in arranging a tow. Weissmuller, who - to confuse the situation further, *had* been able to contact the Union Star only to be referred back to the owners - was asked to wait until proper communications between Union Transport and their troubled vessel had been established. They agreed once more to wait.

Around the coasts of Mount's Bay anyone with access to Channel 16 - fishermen, lifeboatmen, merchantmen in St Ives Bay, police, radio hams, etc - was now aware that a drama was unfolding. They listened to the polite and careful conversations on the radio, listened to the wind in their chimneys, looked into their experience, and sensed an approaching crisis.

At the centre of this complexity, the Union Star wallowed darkly, broadside to the storm. Huge waves, as high as her mast, loomed up suddenly out of the darkness. They broke against her side, cascading across her midships, pressing her far over into the black water, threatening to bury her, then passed under her, lifting her high in the air and whipping her sickeningly over into the next trough to start again. She was as cold as the water and almost entirely unlit. Down in the engine room, George Sedgwick tried to keep his feet on the metal floor and the tools in his hands. With the frequent assistance of the captain he checked his way through all the possible causes of the engine failure. As he re-checked the fuel lines, breaking open joint after joint, quantities of diesel began to swill round the bilges. The two crewmen helped wherever they could. Whittaker stayed on the bridge to take over command whenever needed. Moreton needed to be all things to everyone - a co-ordinator for the rescue effort - a comforter for his wife and children - a mechanic in the engine room.

But at least by 19.00 he knew what his problem was. By steady elimination, expensive in time and effort, they had been forced to look at the quality of the fuel entering the engines. Once they looked, the thin bubbly mixture showed them at once a huge level of water pollution, probably still in progress. The Union Star couldn't possibly run on that. Their task was then straightforward in theory if huge in scope. They had to close off the port tanks, either drain or bypass the daily service tank, check, empty and clean every section of fuel pipe, lead in clean fuel from the starboard tanks, bleed out any air bubbles throughout the system, start a generator to replenish the compressed air tanks, turn the main engines, and off they could go.

In ideal port conditions this would take them a good couple of hours. Somehow they had to achieve it in the pitching semi-darkness in less than that, or lose their ship and possibly their lives as well.

At 19.01 Roberts in Falmouth finally got a call through to the *Union Star*. A precious hour had gone by, and effectively nothing had happened. It was high time to sort the situation out.

BELOW: MOUSEHOLE – THE SMALL FISHING VILLAGE WHICH PROVIDED THE CREW OF THE PENLEE
LIFEBOAT *SOLOMON BROWNE*.

THREE

———

The call was made on a telephone link not on radio, and was not recorded. Roberts' recollection of the call was as follows. He began by expressing his misgivings about the current situation, and said he had a radar echo 4.8kms (3 miles) to the north of where Moreton thought he was. In Roberts' view it was time to shift the rescue efforts up a gear.

The next "gear" in rescue terms is known as a Pan broadcast. This is a general announcement to whoever might be listening that there is a vessel in difficulties and inviting a response from anyone who thinks they can help. It is defined as: "Urgent help required but not in imminent danger." The next level up from Pan is Mayday: "Grave and imminent danger" - usually issued in desperate situations. Protocols and prerogatives are forgotten with Mayday and every available rescue service responds at once, whether requested or not.

Roberts did not think that Moreton would agree to upgrading the situation to Mayday, however much it might simplify matters. He suggested Pan, and Moreton agreed - reluctantly according to Roberts. They also agreed that it was time to get the helicopter airborne. Roberts asked how things were going in the engine room, and Moreton informed him for the first time of the water in the fuel. For Roberts, that was that. He blurted out "Well that's an engine re-start out." Moreton did not respond. Whatever the coastguard thought, he was not ready to write off the Union Star yet. He mentioned that he had set things in motion regarding a tow.

The wording of the Pan broadcast was agreed and the conversation petered out.

Roberts called the Plymouth co-ordination centre and asked them to pass on a request for the helicopter to scramble. Trevelyan Richards was also contacted again directly. He had been waiting at home but had heard nothing for an hour. He was told of the Union Star's plight and the call for the helicopter, but not of the radar plots. He obediently agreed to wait for further news.

Shortly afterwards the next radar plot arrived from the faithful Buckfield. All three contacts had moved, but only the one nearest the coast showed a consistent drift pattern

Meanwhile, the inter-office diplomacy had finally reached a conclusion. Fisher had managed to contact the Union Star and heard the whole sorry story. Without hesitation he authorised Moreton to accept assistance from the Noord Holland as soon as possible. He then received a call from Weissmuller, and officially accepted Lloyds Open Form without demur.

Now 'official', Captain Buurman called Falmouth for the Union Star's latest position. Astonished to find him already under way, Falmouth supplied the position, and they worked out an estimated arrival time, which was included in the Pan broadcast finally issued at twenty past seven. The radar position was not included.

19.20
PAN PAN.

Union Star 14.4km (9 miles) east of the Wolf Rock. Complete engine failure. Eight persons on board. Tug *Noord Holland* proceeding, ETA two hours. Request vessel to stand by.

The results were hardly encouraging. Some ten minutes later the oil-tanker, *Esso Mersey*, called in. She was about 24km (15 miles) to the west, hove-to, and content just to keep her head up in the awful conditions. His ETA was later than Buurman's, and so his offer was politely declined. No one else responded.

Mike Sutherland, the deputy launching authority at Penlee (whose phone had failed to ring at the start of the emergency), had finally become aware of the drama via a chance conversation between his wife and Mrs Madron. He rang Stephen, with whom he had been working earlier, and confirmed that the alert was still on. He then rang Falmouth, who gave him a brief situation report and assured him that everything was safely in hand. Sutherland was the Pilot on duty for the ports of Penzance and Newlyn, and he was hoping to take a ship out when the weather moderated, so he left his office number and went back to work. He assumed that one of the other Penlee officers was overseeing the alert, and did not imagine that Trevelyan alone had been informed of it. He also was not told of the radar reports.

PENLEE POINT LIFEBOAT STATION.

So the second hour ticked by in an air of anxiety but restraint. Every 15 minutes Buckfield's contact moved steadily coastwards, but it was like a bad dream no one wanted to believe. The coastguards still did not feel the situation warranted an all-out rescue operation against the wishes of the captain, with which he might not even co-operate. The lifeboat remained dark and dry in Penlee boathouse. The men, scattered around the village - not huddled around the lifeboat as the coastguards imagined - remained alert, waiting for the phone call or the sound of the signal rockets.

As the social activity of the last Saturday before Christmas gathered pace, people went out for their evening's entertainment unaware of any crisis. For a select few the tension rose and rose, but nothing else happened.

And then, at ten to eight, the waiting was over.

The crew of the Sea King helicopter, code no. R80, had made their way from their homes around Helston to the air base, had changed and received a preliminary briefing. The captain was Lt. Commander Russell Smith, USN, an American on exchange from the US Navy. The remainder of the crew consisted of Co-pilot Ken Docherty, Observer Martin Kennie, and Winchman Steven Marlow. There was no sense of urgency. The weather at Culdrose was rough but not unusually so and the request was to take off women and children only, not abandon ship. There was no Mayday, no-one was sinking or apparently even in immediate danger. The scramble request did not even reach the crew until 19.20 and it was a further seventeen minutes before they were airborne. Falmouth alerted the *Union Star* and told them to have a red flare ready. Moreton had already thought of that.

R80's trip across the bay was short but impressive. The storm seemed to intensify for every yard they flew westwards. They had set off in a mean wind speed of about forty knots, but soon it was sixty-plus, with gusts up to eighty. It was dark and moonless, raining heavily. They reduced height to about 120 metres (400ft), where they were startled to encounter sea-spray. The sea, as far as they could make it out, was equally impressive, with waves up to 12 metres (40ft) high. In just over ten minutes they were in the search area. They were still working on Moreton's original breakdown position as reported in the Pan, and had heard his opinion that the *Union Star* was hardly drifting in at all. However, just as they reached this position, Moreton's red flare shone out through the rain. It was far closer to the shore than they had expected, and Russell Smith whistled and veered off sharply landwards. At 19.50, they sighted the coaster for the first time and sent in the first corroborated report of her position. It was almost exactly where Buckfield's 'Echo A' had indicated, drifting steadily in, and was now just two miles from the point of Tater Du Lighthouse.

19.50

<u>Falmouth Coastguard to *Union Star*:</u> Can you confirm your engine is still u/s, over?
<u>*Union Star* to Falmouth Coastguard:</u> Yes engines are still u/s at this moment, over.

Roberts finally hit all the buttons. There could be no further doubt Quickly calculating her drift, Roberts estimated that at her present speed the *Union Star* would hit the rocks in an hour and a quarter or thereabouts. In terms of sea-room and safety two miles was nothing on such a night. The lifeboat, if it should be needed, was still lying in the boathouse. No shore rescuers had even been alerted. Suddenly time was very short. Roberts rang Trevelyan Richards and requested an immediate launch. He rang the Mousehole Coastal Rescue Company. He rang Don Buckfield and told him to leave his radar at once and rendezvous at Mousehole with them. He contacted Land's End Radio to re-broadcast the Pan incorporating the accurate position. Then he could do no more except wait anxiously for results.

Trevelyan's mother was finishing off some washing in the kitchen, when her son came in and told her that the coastguards had phoned and called for the lifeboat "Call the crew, and the slip crew," he said "tell them to put the rockets off." With that he rushed out, and the door slammed behind him with the wind.

It was a well-established routine. Mary Richards was a second mother to all Trevelyan's crew, and she was usually the one to call them out. First she rang Stephen Madron, the mechanic, and then the Mousehole British Legion, where Nigel Brockman had gone to watch a ladies' darts match. Crewman Gary Wallis was there also, and left with Brockman. One by one she called the rest or passed on the message until her last call, which was to the Ship Inn and its landlord, Charlie Greenhaugh. When she heard the two explosions of the signal maroons, she knew her task was complete.

In any lifeboat community, the sound of the maroons takes precedence over everything else. The rest of the crew lost no time in leaving their homes. John Blewett was in the middle of his daughter's fifteenth birthday party, and had a heavy cold. Barrie Torrie had settled down to watch the Saturday film, 'The Lost City of Atlantis'. So had Kevin Smith, who was also unfit, recovering from viral pneumonia. Charlie Greenhaugh had one of the busiest nights of the winter before him in the 'Ship'. Nevertheless, they all pulled on their RNLI jerseys, donned coats against the filthy weather, and bade their families goodbye. Some gave lifts to others, and they were all at the boathouse within minutes.

The word went out at the same time to the Coastal Rescue Company. These were friends and drinking companions of the lifeboatmen, in fact several had served a turn on the lifeboat themselves. A couple of them were also in the British Legion and they and the lifeboatmen left together, parting at the door for their different destinations.

ABOVE: TREVELYAN RICHARDS WHO LED THE *SOLOMON BROWNE'S* CREW IN ITS COURAGEOUS RESCUE ATTEMPT.

RIGHT: PENLEE BOATHOUSE.

ROYAL NATIONAL LIFEBOAT INSTITUTION PENLEE BRANCH

Hon Sec: D.L. JOHNSON
Tel. Day Penzance 4345
· Night · 4126
Coxswain · · W.T. RICHARDS
Tel. Mousehole 242
2nd Coxs Mech · J.S. MADRON
Tel. Mousehole 337
Asst. Mechanic N. BROCKMAN
Tel. Mousehole 673
Head Launcher · · D. PENROSE
Tel. Mousehole 386

THE *SOLOMON BROWNE* GOES DOWN THE SLIPWAY IN A FLURRY OF FOAM – A PICTURE TAKEN
JUST TWO WEEKS BEFORE THE DISASTER.

FOUR

The Penlee Lifeboat lay at readiness, as she did night and day, every day of the year. She was a 14.1 metres (47ft) 'Watson' class, a development of a design style which went right back to the early rowing gigs and whalers. Like them, she had graceful lines and a porpoise-like hull, well used to taking water on deck. She was made of double-planked mahogany, with twin screws set in tunnels for their own protection, equipped with the latest in navigational and radio equipment, and painted in the traditional orange and blue of the RNLI. Most of the money for the lifeboat's construction had been left in her will by one Elizabeth Mary Dyer Browne, and she named it in memory of her father, a squire from Landrake in East Cornwall, Solomon Browne.

Cars arrived on the road above, boots clattered down the steps at the rear, and the lights were switched on. The boathouse quickly began to fill up. Three kinds of people flock to a lifeboat launch: the regular crew, the launching crew with established duties in the boathouse, and the other would-be helpers or crewmembers, affectionately known as 'runners'. Regular crew members are often away at sea themselves, and might be ill or otherwise absent, and the runners come in the hope of filling any gaps in the lifeboat's complement. Most of the crew had started as runners themselves. To serve in the lifeboat is a great honour, especially amongst the young, and competition is always keen.

However, it was no night for the inexperienced. The wind was tearing across the open bay, pushing up huge seas before it, and the storm was still only a shadow of what it was to become. Rain and spray was drumming on the boathouse roof. The regular crew started arriving, picking up their lifejackets and climbing straight on board, carefully checking each other's clothing and equipment. Trevelyan was one of the first to arrive and noted with satisfaction that nearly all of his 'first team' were present.

Stephen Madron was 35, and as mechanic he was the crew's only paid employee of the RNLI, although he also worked as boatman to the local pilots. He was also second coxswain, in command when Trevelyan was away. His connection with the Penlee lifeboat went back at least three generations, and his grandfather Edwin had been awarded a Silver Medal as coxswain for his rescue of the passage crew of the battleship HMS *Warspite* in 1947. An affable and gregarious man, he was married with a young son and daughter.

Nigel Brockman, 43, was assistant mechanic. He was a fish salesman with the firm of BJ Ridge in Newlyn, although he still did some fishing of his own. He was renowned for his mischief and irreverent wit, and stories of his exploits as a joker abound. He was married with three teenage sons, and had been a crew member for sixteen years.

John Blewett was a quieter type, though not above some fun. Aged 43, he came from an old Mousehole family and was closely involved in most village activities One of his most important positions was as electrician for the famous Mousehole Christmas lights, where his skill as a British Telecom engineer came in very useful. He lived in the village where he was born with his wife and two children.

Barry Torrie was a fisherman of 33, who had been on the crew since his teens. The Torries had lived in Mousehole ever since an ancestor had been wrecked on St Clement's Island and had come ashore to found a dynasty. Barrie too was born in the village, and was now married with two young sons.

Kevin Smith was 23 and had moved to Mousehole from Yorkshire with his family in his early teens. He was obsessed by the sea, and had been a 'runner' ever since he arrived. Trevelyan liked him, and he achieved a regular place at a very early age. He was a seaman aboard the Cunard liner *Samaria* at home on leave.

Smith's friend Gary Wallis was 22, a Londoner whose family had also settled in the village. He also was a fisherman working out of Newlyn, and had worked his way onto the regular lifeboat crew by sheer persistence. He also still lived with his family.

Trevelyan Richards himself - known to everyone as 'Charlie' - was 56, and a legend. His authority over the lifeboat was undisputed. Like many of his generation in the village, he had been on and off boats since he could walk, and lived for the sea. He started his career as a boy crew on a crabber, and worked his way up to skipper of a trawler. He had been in charge of the trawler *Excellent* for many years. His lifeboat service began on the old 'W & S' in 1950, ten years before the *Solomon Browne* was built. Eventually, he was chosen as coxswain, and he was held in deep respect by all the crew for his experience and skill. His word was law and he could be a hard task-master, but he too had his boyish side, and under his command the Penlee crew had a reputation not only as a formidable lifeboat team, but also as a bunch of men who knew how to enjoy themselves.

On a night such as this the regulation crew for the Watson was eight men. Richards was one short, and he looked over the runners for a suitable volunteer. As usual, despite the conditions, there was no shortage. Nigel Brockman's teenage son, Neil, who was also a fisherman, asked to go, but was turned down. "No more than one from a family on a night like this," said Richards, an unusually solemn remark. Dennis Leslie, a local GP and dedicated lifeboat supporter - hero of dozens of medical call-outs - put himself forward, but Richards turned him down also without ceremony. "Not tonight Doc, you're too old." He looked over the others, several of whom had served in the past. Before he could choose, the burly form of Charlie Greenhaugh suddenly appeared in the boathouse shouting "You're not going without me!"

Greenhaugh, originally from Wallassey, Cheshire, was 46, ex-Royal Navy and Merchant Navy, and now publican. Before *The Ship*, he had been landlord of a pub at Long Rock, near Marazion, for many years. He was a very popular figure, and had been granted the honour of switching on the Christmas lights the night before. No-one contradicted him. "Put up a jacket," smiled Trevelyan, and Greenhaugh took his place on board.

By now the engines were already turning over, and the lifeboat was slowly being hydraulically tipped over from the horizontal to match the angle of the slipway.

William Trevelyan Richards

James Stephen Madron

Nigel Brockman

John Robert Blewett

Charles Thomas Greenhaugh

Kevin Smith

Barrie Robertson Torrie

Gary Lee Wallis

THE CREW OF THE *SOLOMON BROWNE*. THESE PHOTOGRAPHS ARE STILL EXHIBITED IN PENLEE BOATHOUSE.

Dudley Penrose, the head launcher, folded back the two sets of doors and made them fast with some difficulty. The full force of the elements struck those inside the boathouse for the first time. The wind roared into the opening like a wild animal, creating a whirlwind of noise. The waves were cresting over the side of the slipway up to 4.5 - 6 metres (15 - 20ft) high, steep and short, bursting into spray. The meeting point between the slipway and the water was sometimes almost in front of them and sometimes 30 metres (100ft) away and below. If the tide had been fuller, a launch would have been totally impossible. No-one could remember worse conditions, and the crew looked down thoughtfully at the wild confusion they were about to enter.

The lifeboat was slowly lowered out just clear of the boathouse so that the radio and radar masts could be raised.

NEIL BROCKMAN AT 17, WHO WAS TURNED DOWN AS CREW BY TREVELYAN RICHARDS BECAUSE HIS FATHER WAS ALREADY ON BOARD, WAS LATER TO BECOME COXSWAIN OF PENLEE LIFEBOAT HIMSELF.

It was Penrose's task as launcher to knock out the retaining pin with his 21lb hammer to set the lifeboat sliding towards the sea. The timing had to be just right. If a wave caught the lifeboat while still on the slipway it would knock her straight off the other side, onto the rocks below. Penrose stood behind the stern and waited, acutely aware that a false blow could drown the whole crew.

Trevelyan went forward to look at the waves. Then he stood poised, with one foot on the wheelhouse. Everyone waited for the signal. At last a huge sea struck the slipway, foaming up almost to the lifeboat's bows, and as it reached its height the coxswain suddenly chopped down his arm and shouted, "Now!"

Penrose smote out the pin with one clean blow and the *Solomon Browne* started to slide, following the receding wave. She plunged into the water at maximum speed and the momentum carried her clear. As the spray blew away she was already turning hard to starboard to face the next wave. She met it with room to spare, and was away.

The boathouse crew watched her masthead light showing on the crest of wave after wave. They went back up to the road to watch her out of sight. Penrose radioed in the successful launch and the crew list. The boathouse was closed up and the lights turned off. There was nothing to do now but wait.

OPPOSITE: THE *SOLOMON BROWNE* AT SEA.

FIVE

S ea King Rescue 80 hovered as best it could about 30 metres (100ft) astern of the stricken coaster, while the crew gave themselves time to assess the situation. The *Union Star* was a sorry sight, wallowing and rolling about forty degrees, with seas continually breaking over the hatches and on occasions the bridge structure as well.

It was not an encouraging prospect. The superstructure was confined to the rear fifth of the vessel, and even there the space was not designed for easy access from the air. Behind the bridge was a central structure which divided the limited space in half, and around that were lifeboats, winches, ventilators and other obstructions. The most significant feature for the airmen was the mast. It was a two-legged affair, which met at the top in a short central mast and radar aerial. It was designed to fold down under road bridges for river and canal work. The process of folding it down under the prevailing conditions was obviously out of the question, and so somehow they would have to work around it. It was 15 metres (50ft) tall, rising and falling over 9 metres (30ft) with the waves, and at the same time yawing and whipping back with little warning.

From the little choice available, they decided to aim for the starboard side of the after deck, the lee side as she lay. The winchman, Steven Marlow, was on the radio and asked Moreton how many people were coming off. Moreton had no second thoughts - only the woman and children were to leave. Without further ado Marlow, who was already in his harness, handed over the radio and radar, opened the big hatch door, and with the assistance of Martin Kennie, the winch-operator, lowered himself out into the screaming air.

In his standard immersion suit, Marlow was well insulated from the wind and rain, and was able to remain relatively comfortable while on the sling. He found himself in a strange three-dimension world with absolutely no fixed points. Below him the *Union Star* rose and swung and fell in the most extreme manner. Above him the Sea King tried to maintain a steady hover, but the gusts were terrific and unpredictable. The helicopter was blown back initially with each gust, and since unfortunately these died without warning as suddenly as they arose, it tended to leap forward when the wind dropped again. The wind caught Marlow too and tried to fling him through the air. He swung through huge irregular arcs, unable to tell which force was moving him where.

Below he saw a man emerge from the bridge with a female, though whether it was the mother or one of the daughters Marlow could not tell. The crewman held the female against one of the lockers to steady them both and prevent them being washed away. R80 came in for its first attempt at a transfer. Kennie, on the winch, had the task of trying to land Marlow safely on the deck with the winch while keeping the pilot - who had a far inferior view - informed via the internal radio which way he wanted him to go.

A ROYAL NAVY SEA KING HELICOPTER ON ROUTINE CASUALTY TRANSFER EXERCISE WITH
A LIFEBOAT.

The Sea King gives little impression of its true size when seen in flight. It is in fact a bulky and substantial aircraft, nearly 5 metres (17ft) tall, and, 17.3 metres (57ft) long, 3 metres (10ft) longer than the *Solomon Browne*. The most important vital statistics for the pilot, however, relate to the rotors. The main rotor has a diameter of 18.8 metres (62ft), and when the overhang of the main blade is added to the protrusion of the rear stabilising rotor, his aircraft is effectively 22.2 metres (73ft) long and 18.8 metres (62ft) wide. A blow, a snag, a touch from anything solid into that pattern of airspace spells instant certain death.

Russell Lewis Smith, 34, was a Lieutenant-Commander in the United States Navy who had been for two years on an exchange tour with the Royal Navy. He was a highly experienced Sea King pilot, both in military and Search-and-Rescue duties, and had already taken part in a number of real-life rescues. All his experience was needed to try to cope with the intense gusting which made steady hovering so difficult. The pilot sits with both hands and both feet fully engaged, regulating the helicopter's three-way movement - up and down, forward and back, side to side. Smith had his side window open and gazed down at the casualty over his right shoulder, while co-pilot Ken Docherty beside him gazed ahead, trying to anticipate the squalls. Docherty and Kennie were both continually feeding information to their skipper through throat-mikes, guiding him to the ideal position and warning him of waves, wind, and the masts of the coaster. The noise from the rotors and the wind was deafening. It was relentless and exhausting work.

The crew of a rescue helicopter need to have absolute faith and trust in each other, particularly the winchman and winch operator. The operator controls a piece of vulnerable humanity on the end of a wire, and the winchman depends on his skill not to throw him against the ship or its masts, not to land him too fast or onto a dangerous obstruction, and not - if at all possible - to give him an unnecessary ducking.

Marlow swung through the air as though on a giant trapeze, watching the ship coming closer. He liked to pick a fixed spot and concentrate on it to orientate himself when about to land. He looked down. The Sea King had all its lights on, two in the nose, two downward facing lights in the side sponsons and a controllable spotlight. Marlow noticed the shoes the female was wearing. They were an unexpected shocking pink against the green decking. He kept his eyes fixed on them as he neared the deck. Kennie lowered him further as R80 crept up behind the *Union Star*. He was wearing a double harness, so that he could be raised together with each casualty and help to keep them calm and steady in the air. There was a crucial point where Marlow reached the level of the highest point of the *Union Star's* swing. Then the timing had to be perfect, because the coaster was moving very fast for such a solid object and could have crushed the winchman with one blow.

The first attempt was all wrong, so they broke off and came straight back again. Once more they inched upwind at right-angles to the stern. This time Marlow swung to within 3 - 4.5 metres (10 - 15ft) of the deck, which was close, but not close enough. Again they broke off and came around. The third time Smith came in a little lower, trying to make up the difference. They were all concentrating on the winchman. Suddenly a larger wave threw the *Union Star* over onto her side. As she rolled back, her mast lurched suddenly upwards. Kennie shouted a warning, but it was too late for evasive action. The top of the mast shot up, reached its zenith and dropped into the next trough. It had missed the main rotors by less than 3 metres (10ft). Considerably shaken, the crew winched Marlow back inside and stood off for re-assessment.

The obvious alternative was another technique, the 'high line' method. This involved passing a guideline to the crew of the vessel, which they could hold onto but not tie fast. The winchman would then be lowered on his own line as before, using the high line to guide himself down to the deck. There were two distinct advantages to this method, firstly that it eliminated the free swinging which was proving so dangerous, and secondly it meant that the helicopter could stand off to the side and let the winch man slide down the angle rather than having to hover directly above the vessel. It required the intelligent co-operation of the ship's crew, which could be difficult where there was a language barrier, but it seemed ideal in these circumstances. Smith called up Moreton on the radio and briefed him on what to do. Moreton had news of his own.

20.08

R80 to Union Star: Suggest you leave all lights on that you are able to.
Union Star to R80: Yes, we have just managed to get the generator started. I'll put some lights on for you and see how it goes.

It was true. To Sedgwick's credit he had managed to clean the lines to one of auxiliary generators and start it up. The effect on the Union Star's morale was magical. As all the electrical circuits came back, Moreton started to replenish the compressed air bottles which were needed to start the main engines. The ship began to hum with returning life. He switched on the deck lights, which flooded the scene with bright halogen light. Hope returned with the power. It might be close, but it seemed they would make it yet.

The high line was ready. The first task was to trail it across the Union Star's stern so that one of the crewmen could grab it. A man came out and stood ready by the coaster's stern, while the helicopter approached as slowly and smoothly as it was able. The line crept towards the ship and trailed across the deck between the man on the stern and the other two. Smith struggled to hold position. The line was only about 1 metre from the man yet he made no attempt to take it. Eventually Smith had to break off and circle round to start again.

They repeated this manoeuvre six times.

They had one success. On one perfect approach, they actually trailed the line directly to the man on the stern, who caught it. For a moment the rescue was on. But just as he did so, the Union Star fell into one of the spectacular 9 metres (30ft) troughs and the line jerked out of his hands. Frustrated by inaction, Marlow had himself lowered about 4.5 metres (15ft) to try to steady the line but all the other attempts were just near-misses. On the final run the mast threatened them again, this time by entangling the high line. Marlow managed to free the line from his position in mid-air, but it was their second brush with disaster and once more they were forced to stand off and re-assess.

Channel 16 had been quiet during this period of concentrated action, but now it filled again, with the sound of highly experienced and professional men beginning to realise that the situation might be beyond them.

20.24

<u>R80 to *Union Star*:</u> Too difficult for us as far as safety is concerned. We're getting very close to your mast and we don't have a long enough line.
<u>*Union Star* to R80:</u> OK. Very much obliged for your assistance. Going to put an anchor down.

Moreton's radar was back on, and he could no longer enjoy any delusions about his position or rate of drift. On the other hand his conviction that the *Union Star* could be saved was stronger than ever. He was now less than a mile from the rocks, and urgently needed to buy some time. The anchors were hardly likely to be equal to the situation, but they had to be tried.

The only way to lower the anchor was to go forward to the anchor locker and knock out the retaining pin. In normal conditions, it was a routine task. To go forward from the bridge in the current conditions would be an heroic venture. The ship's roll swung each rail high into the air then plunged it deep into the water, while the waves swept across the hatches like a reef. Nonetheless one of the crew succeeded in making this fraught journey at least once and probably twice. The starboard anchor ran out, engaged a solid object on the sea bed, and parted like a rotten thread. The port anchor was then lowered with more success, to the length of four shackles. Though it could not hold the ship, it dragged fairly slowly, and cut down her shoreward momentum.

The more dramatic effect of this was seen from above, as the *Union Star* suddenly slewed to port and held position, bow-on to the sea. Every larger wave now buried the fo'c'sle and rolled along the hatches, to explode in spray against the bridge. The ship shuddered with the impact. As Moreton called in to report dropping anchor, even his uncannily calm tones were tinged with fear.

The helicopter crew were trying to lengthen their high line, to give themselves more room to operate. They had found another length of line of lighter gauge, but it was tangled. They spread it over the broad hold of the Sea King and spent precious time trying to sort it out. While they were trying to untangle and tie on the extra line, they radioed Moreton with their intentions and checked once again how many people he wanted taken off. The answer was still the same: "One woman and two children".

After several minutes of frustration it became clear to them that the second line was so light that it would merely stream out behind them in the wind, giving no extra advantage. The cold realisation began to sink in that although only 27 metres (30 yds) above the eight people in the *Union Star*, some of whose faces they could clearly see looking through the windows of the wheelhouse, they had really no idea how to save them.

But by now other help was arriving.

SIX

The *Noord Holland* and the Penlee lifeboat arrived on the scene at almost the same time. Buurman checked in first, having been standing back to observe for several minutes. Perhaps mindful of the strained nature of their last conversation, Buurman's initial greeting to Moreton was - even for him - a masterpiece of the laconic.

20.43

Noord Holland to Union Star: Noord Holland to Union Star.
Union Star to Noord Holland: Reading you loud and clear skip.
Noord Holland to Union Star: Roger ... er, you want a tow or something?

They discussed the situation calmly. Buurman said he was most concerned that the woman and children should come off first, and he did not want to come in and hamper the helicopter's movements. He also pointed out that passing a tow to the Union Star would be very difficult. He did his best to let Moreton down easily.

20.45

Noord Holland to Union Star: Wait until the woman and children are off, then we'll have a closer look and see what we can do. We hope the best, over.
Union Star to Noord Holland: Yep fair enough then skip, yeh, OK then.

In fact, there was nothing a closer look could tell Buurman, except what he already knew. His first look showed him clearly that his harrowing journey had been a waste of time.

Tugs can perform miracles in taking ships in tow in bad conditions, but they need plenty of sea-room. They also like to approach from the lee side. Buurman could not do this without going into the breakers amongst the rocks and shoals, and it was already quite hazardous enough where he was.

The anchor was another factor. The *Union Star's* bows were now plunging deeply into every wave, and no one could expect to go forward on her and live. This meant that no one could fix the tow-line, and no-one could knock out the anchor which would drag against the tow. Also Buurman's radar was unserviceable, so he was reduced to visual watches only in visibility which closed in to 274 metres (300 yds) in the squalls.

As soon as he took in the situation there was no doubt in Buurman's mind. Like the helicopter, he could observe and encourage from close range, but there seemed to be no way he could help.

"Yep fair enough then skip, yeh. OK then."

It was a bitter blow for Moreton. He had been counting on the tug as his margin of safety if time ran out. Now for the first time he had to seriously consider that he might lose everything. He did not doubt that, with rescuers on all sides, their lives would somehow be saved, but time and options were getting perilously tight for the *Union Star*.

Shortly afterwards he heard the rasping tones of Trevelyan Richards in his ears.

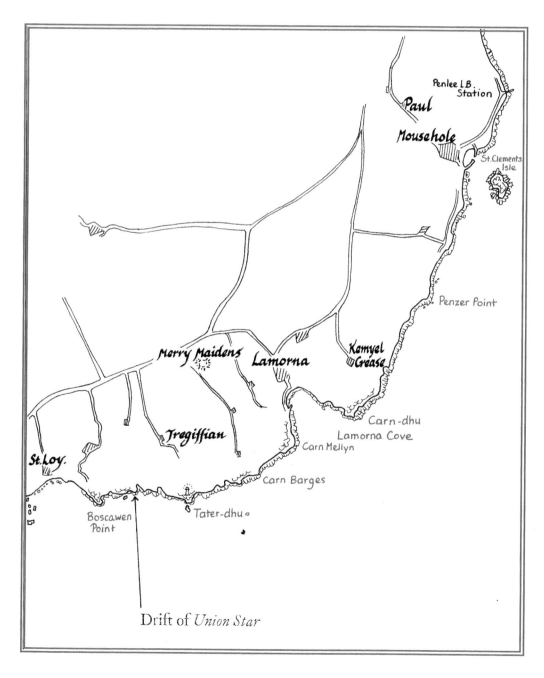

Drift of *Union Star*

The *Solomon Browne* had completed one of the worst journeys in her life, constantly in danger of capsizing, constantly battered and swamped. They had made the 4km (2.5 miles) passage in half an hour, which was good going in such weather. As they rounded Tater Du the crew could see for the first time the extreme hazard of the *Union Star's* position. She was drifting into a shallow bay, bounded by Tater Du to the east and Boscawen Point to the west. The bay was full of shoals and shallows, rocks, half-tide rocks, and rocks which only showed in storms such as this. It was only two hours after low water, not enough to give any reliable depth below the keel.

To go in and engage the coaster would be to enter a trap. Lifeboats, like tugs, prefer to work in from the lee, to gain what protection they can from the larger vessel. Anchored head-on to the seas, the *Union Star* had effectively no lee to offer. The only option was to come alongside in the few seconds' respite between waves, break off to face them, and circle round in great danger to repeat the manoeuvre as often as necessary. Once engaged they would feel committed to keep trying until successful. No one could have blamed the coxswain if he too had concluded that the odds against him were too long, and that he too should stand back.

The moment passed and the question never arose. "You've got to go," as a lifeboat coxswain once said. "You haven't got to come back."

20.47

Penlee Lifeboat to Union Star: Understand you had trouble with the chopper ... do you want for us to come alongside and take the woman and children over?

Moreton had recovered his extraordinary composure.
Union Star to Penlee Lifeboat: Yes please. The helicopter is having a bit of difficulty getting to us, so if you could pop out ... I'll be very much obliged over.

However, before anyone could pop anywhere, R80 decided to have another go with the high line as it was. Richards agreed to keep out of the way for the time being. Once again the crewman went out onto the stern of the *Union Star* to wait.

Gingerly, highly aware of the mast-head, Smith made another pass towards the coaster, trying to work a diagonal to avoid flying directly over the ship. The weight-bag at the end of the line dipped into the water. As it did so a huge early-breaking wave curled up and crashed down on top of it. When the wave passed the weight-bag had gone and the line streamed out uselessly in the wind. For a moment the helicopter crew gaped in disbelief - the breaking strength of the line was 182kg (400lb) - then they had to admit defeat.

20.54

R80 to Penlee Lifeboat: That's it for us. Will stand off in case you need us.

The *Union Star* was no more than 457 metres (500 yds) from the shore. All else having failed, the 47' Watson and the eight volunteers from Mousehole were now all that remained between those aboard and destruction. Almost three hours after Moreton's first report, the *Solomon Browne* closed in for the first time.

As they approached, the *Solomon Browne* contacted the *Union Star* by radio to let them know they were aiming for their port side, and to make something else clear.

20.57

<u>Penlee Lifeboat to *Union Star*:</u> ... advise you with crew everybody to come off over.

The mate was on the R/f and had none of Moreton's airs or illusions.

<u>*Union Star* to Penlee Lifeboat:</u> Yes we're all coming off.

Easier said, however, than done.

As they came further into the shallows, the waves were forced up, higher and steeper. The most conservative estimates put them at 10.6 - 12.1 metres (35 - 40ft), as tall as a four-storey building and almost as high as the *Solomon Browne* was long. The wind was sufficient to blow a man over, and the rain stung the face like gravel. Richards brought the *Solomon Browne* in as gently as he could to the port side, facing to seaward. Excepting the coxswain, engineer and radio operator, all the rest of the crew were on deck, lifelines clipped on, and holding heavy grappling ropes in their hands. The vessels collided with some force while the lifeboat was at the coaster's midships. As soon as they touched, the crewmen threw the lines over the *Union Star's* rail to hold position for as long as possible. They waved to the crew on the bridge urging them to make a run for it. Within seconds the next wave reared up at them out of the darkness and the lifeboat had to break off quickly to tackle it unencumbered. This made her lose position and she had to wear round again, taking what opportunities she could to turn between crests, avoiding a capsize. She then had to repeat the whole manoeuvre.

R80 stood directly above, drifting in with the *Union Star* to shine as much light as possible and observe.

No one emerged from the bridge.

Still held by the port anchor, the coaster was bucking and rearing like a wild animal on a rope, yawing from side to side. Her bows dipped into the oncoming waves and water rushed up the decks to the bridge. Looking down, the eight people – Sedgwick presumably having been finally called away from his uncompleted task - tried to calculate how to get to the lifeboat in the few seconds available. It was only a few metres from the rear door around to the metal steps and along the side decks, but wind, the spray and the motion of the boat made it desperately dangerous. And who was to go first? Probably five fit and experienced seamen, desperate for their lives, could have made the journey safely, with luck. But they could not abandon Mrs Moreton and the girls. They had been adrift for three hours, and were cold, seasick, terrified, battered and exhausted. The deck where they had played the day before was now a maelstrom and the *Solomon Browne* looked infinitely tiny and fragile. Humanity and custom dictated that they should be rescued first, and the captain last. No crewman could precede the womenfolk. They in turn would be unwilling to leave without the captain. The abandon-ship would therefore have to be a well-disciplined simultaneous operation, and this required time and organisation which they simply did not have.

The lifeboat tried a different technique, drifting slowly down the side from seaward, probably using the drogue, or sea anchor. This time she aimed for the higher afterdeck behind the bridge. The waves were becoming more complex and unpredictable as the effect of the shallows and the backwash from the surrounding cliffs combined to confuse the picture. Smaller waves could suddenly arise from any quarter. The *Solomon Browne* was thrown hard against the Union Star's side time after time, with force that would have damaged a normal vessel. The Watson was designed with such encounters in mind, and was not afraid to come in close.

If the side decks were too low, the after-deck was a little too high for easy access. The relative movement of the two vessels was not predictable and no-one could tell when the two decks might line up for a few seconds. Several times the Solomon Browne drifted down the side of the coaster and every time the crew held on with their ropes and waved at the white faces they could see on the bridge. But the people they were risking their lives for could see no safe way to reach them, and could only wave uselessly back.

Frustration set in. One of the Union Star's crew slipped out and let out a rope ladder from the side of the afterdeck, but no one took the suicidal step of actually going down it. One of the Mousehole men decided to sort matters out for himself and made a determined attempt to cross over to the Union Star, presumably to haul them out in person if necessary. He was pulled back, either by the ship's movement or by his friends. On one run down the side, with the bows nosing in towards the Union Star's side, an unexpected wave threw her up so that her front quarter landed over the rail onto the side decking, with an impact which made her mast head light go off. She quickly clawed back into the water and carried on as if nothing had happened.

The distance between them and the shore closed inexorably. At 21.05, Russell Smith called to warn that they were about 183 metres (200 yds) from the cliff. He estimated they had ten minutes left.

Smith was concerned for his own position also. He had radar and bearings from Tater Du's light, and knew he was backing slowly into a trap. Although it was blazing with every light they possessed - including even the Aldis lamp - crucially the Sea King had no lights pointing to the rear. The tail rotor projected behind, and would be the first thing to touch the cliffs if they were blown back too far. One touch and they were dead. Although the radar showed them the line of the shore, it did not show the shape of the cliff, whether a slope or a sheer wall. They only knew that it was 91.4 metres (300ft) high, and they were hovering at 30 metres (100ft).

The wind was now gusting to 160kmph (100 miles per hour) and on occasions they could not help being blown backwards. Marlow and Kennie peered desperately into the mist and spray. They had been told that a Coastguard Rescue Company was standing by on the shore, and they tried to make out the lights which should be shining towards them. That would show them exactly how much margin of safety they had left. But they gazed in vain.

SEVEN

In response to the urgent summons from Falmouth, Don Buckfield had left his radar set at Land's End at 19.55 and had set off in the coastguard Land Rover. It was fitted with radio and as he drove he checked with Falmouth the best place for his crew to muster. Buckfield's own plot had shown 'Echo A' moving fairly steadily towards the point of Tater Du, but he checked to see if the helicopter's sighting confirmed this.

There is good road access to the coast at Tater Du and again at Lamorna Cove. The coastline between them does not look far on a map but, as anyone who has walked it knows, it rises and falls, twists and turns, going from rocky crags almost down to the waterline, precipitous in places and very exposed to the weather.

Buckfield asked for confirmation of Tater Du as a mustering point, but to his surprise Falmouth suggested that Lamorna looked the better bet. He checked again, but the answer was still the same. Since Falmouth was in a position to know, Buckfield quibbled no further. Lamorna it would be.

Buckfield sped to Mousehole to organise the crew and found them loading equipment at the coastguard hut into a builder's lorry loaned for the occasion. He gave a hand and then set off for Lamorna together with others following in cars. They arrived and parked on the harbour, and Buckfield had a close look at the size of the waves that were funnelling into the Cove. Looking out to sea, he could see no sign of the casualty, helicopter or lifeboat. He quickly mustered an advance party - Doug Hoare, his son Richard Hoare, and Mike Buttery - to explore around to the west and pinpoint the scene of the crisis, with lights, rockets and a mobile radio.

The path climbs steeply out of Lamorna to the west, rising about 91.4 metres (300ft) to the point of Carn Mellyn, and as they came out of the cove the weather hit the advance party with full force. Wind, rain and spray beat upon them. The rain had turned the path into a river, and it was dark, steep and treacherous. They had not gone far before it became apparent that Doug Hoare was in difficulties, unable to keep up. They decided that he should stay in a sheltered place while the other two went ahead at their own pace. They rushed on as fast as they dared in the pitch darkness.

As they came up to the next point, Carn Barges, they were mystified. By now they could just see the lights of the *Noord Holland* out at sea, but although Buttery could hear all the sounds of rescue attempts in progress on the mobile radio, they could now see all the way to Tater Du Lighthouse and should - by their information - be able to see everything that was going on. They could see nothing. And then, to their absolute astonishment, the lights of the *Solomon Browne* suddenly appeared from behind the point of Tater Du. Buttery swore aloud. Not only was the lifeboat to the west of the lighthouse, but also she seemed suicidally close to shore in the conditions. At least she was heading out to sea at first, but as they watched the red navigation light changed to green. Buttery shouted, "Bloody hell, look, the lifeboat's about" and as he did, the lights slipped out of sight again inside the point, into the shallow bay behind.

Buttery got straight onto the radio. Using his code name, he informed Buckfield in no uncertain terms that the action was taking place to the west of Tater Du, not the east, and that Buckfield had better get round there, not omitting to add that it would have made more sense if they had all gone there in the first place.

Buckfield had been waiting in Lamorna with the rest of the crew, their only diversion being to move the vehicles from the front car park before the rising tide allowed the waves to actually wash them away. His own Land Rover had been particularly difficult to start. He too cursed in turn when he heard Buttery's news. There was little point in recalling the advance crew now, but clearly someone had to get to Tater Du as fast as possible. He decided to leave the rest of the Mousehole crew to pack up again, and go at once the long way round the roads in the Land Rover. As he left, he called Falmouth to summon the cliff rescue teams from Sennen and St Levan to rendezvous with him at the lighthouse.

Back at Carn Barges, Buttery and Hoare caught their breath, and then plunged onwards again along the narrow path as fast as they were able.

A couple of miles to the west of them a local fisherman by the name of Mike Townsend was also converging on the lighthouse from the other direction. He lived in the beautiful cove of St Loy, and had been listening-in on Channel 16 from home. Soon he could see as well as hear, as the Union Star's lights together with the Sea King, and the Noord Holland's searchlight lit the night sky. He could stay at home no longer and set off eastwards along the same coast-path. He knew the coast well enough, and reckoned that the Union Star was doomed, but he was very concerned to see the lifeboat still making runs at her so close to shore. As he stumbled along, the bulk of Carn Boscawen blocked out the scene.

Two witnesses were even closer, a telephone engineer and a journalist.

Leon Pezzack was an engineer for British Telecom. He was a Mousehole man, friend and companion of most of the lifeboat crew. John Blewett, the emergency mechanic, had been his best friend since their schooldays and his Best Man. At about the time the Union Star was breaking down, he had had a report of a loose cable on the lane down to Tater Du. However, since the lighthouse was working satisfactorily, he was advised to wait until daylight to investigate. When he heard the maroons go off, Pezzack immediately thought again of the lighthouse. He heard about the drifting coaster, and decided to go out to Tater Du at once and check that all was really well. Tater Du was automatic and unmanned, and he could not bear the thought that it might be malfunctioning during a crisis at sea. He drove out and started checking the lines from the top of Tregiffian Lane. At the bottom, he became aware of the sound of a helicopter over the gale. She seemed to be under the cliff at the bottom of the lane, showing lights. He went straight down, noted that the lighthouse was functioning correctly, and then gave all his attention to the extraordinary scene below.

It was about 20.55, and the lifeboat had just started making runs at the Union Star. As Pezzack watched, she fired a white flare to illuminate a particularly dangerous ledge. As the flare died she came alongside the coaster. The blaze of light around her contrasted with the intense darkness behind and made it seem like a stage, with the three main players. The lights shone into the water and through the waves, so that they looked light green and phosphorescent. Pezzack watched while his friends repeatedly set the lifeboat against the coaster. He estimated they were about 228 metres (250 yds) from the cliffs, and coming in fast.

Andrew Besley was a photographer, journalist, and stringer for a number of national papers. He kept a barograph at his home near St Ives, and early that evening he had noticed it performing the quickest decline he had ever seen. Checking around his contacts to see if there was anything newsworthy in the storm, he heard about the *Union Star's* predicament. He arrived at Mousehole, stopping at Penlee just after the lifeboat had launched, and he watched her lights disappearing. Besley asked one of the launching crew where the casualty was, and was told it was probably at Tater Du. With his son he drove westwards on the coast road directly to Tater Du. Unlike the official rescue services, they quickly found themselves right where the action was. They stood up as well as they could against the gale, and watched the lifeboat's first rescue attempts. After a while Besley was concerned by the lack of the journalist's other limb, the telephone, and sent his son off back to the farm to beg the use of theirs.

The watchers were unaware of each other, but they were only a few metres apart on the lane below Tregiffian Cottages. From this point there are one or two overgrown fields before the cliff edge, and so the first 45 metres (50 yds) or so from the shore are hidden from view. It was too dark for photography, and Besley did not wait until the ships disappeared before following his son, to alert the wider world. His impression as he left was that the *Solomon Browne* had broken off the rescue attempt. Pezzack remained in his van with the lights off and the windscreen wipers on and observed for several minutes longer.

THE REAR DECK AREA OF THE SISTER SHIP *UNION MARS* SHOWING THE RESTRICTED SPACE AND MANY OBSTRUCTIONS.

Quiet, polite radio messages were still passing between the three craft at the heart of the incident. Moreton asked if Richards thought they should take to a life raft, but Trevelyan told him to stay put.

"OK Skip, yep", said Moreton. After that he listened only, and did not speak again.

Watching the crew of the *Solomon Browne* risking their lives again and again just below them without response was finally too much for the Culdrose men. They were young, and courageous, and could no longer stand the frustration of observing without taking part. They decided to have one more desperate - foolhardy - attempt with the ordinary transfer harness, the manoeuvre they had broken off as too dangerous an hour earlier. Smith spoke to Trevelyan and they agreed to make simultaneous rescue runs. He then brought Sea King R80 down and down once again to within range of the deck, and within reach of the thrashing mast. Again Marlow went out of the door and into the elements.

The conditions were infinitely worse than before. The wind was higher, the gusts were extreme, and the waves had increased to unreal proportions; Smith reckoned them up to 18.2 metres (60ft) high. As they closed once again with the *Union Star*, the mast sliced through the air towards them and passed within a short distance of the rotor. They quickly winched Marlow back in, but still they would not give up. Smith gained height and Marlow went out yet again, to the length of about 4.5 metres (15ft). The helicopter settled back down one last time over the jumping coaster. Suddenly Kennie yelled a warning and Smith kicked the controls as hard as he could. This time Kennie reckoned that no more than 1 metre (3ft) had separated the masthead from the rotor blade as it sailed past. Temporarily out of control the Sea King was flung backwards, 25 or 30 metres (30-40 yds). They all tensed, waiting for the impact. On the wire Marlow tossed and jumped like a yo-yo. The gust threw him violently upwards and he struck one of the sponsons, denting it with his shoulder. It probably saved him from the rotor.

Smith regained control and Marlow was recovered, bruised but safe, inside. There really was nothing else they could do, and Smith gained some height while the four of them continued to observe, very lucky indeed to be still alive.

Below the lifeboat continued to circle and contact. Like a terrier nothing could shake her off for long, and the men in the helicopter were awed by her persistence. But still no one came out. Matters seemed to have reached an impasse, which would only be resolved by Boscawen cliffs.

Then without any warning the over-stressed anchor chain finally parted. With the next wave the *Union Star* yawed violently back to her original position, beam-on to the seas, bows to the west. Every wave threatened to roll her over, and she was quickly driven towards the line of breakers.

Still the *Solomon Browne* pursued her. Although an approach from the lee side was now out of the question, the new position marginally improved the chances of taking people off, if only there was time. She ran in twice as the coaster neared the breakers. The first attempt came to nothing. On the second their amazing luck and skill finally ran out. A wave caught the lifeboat on her approach, tossed her high in the air, and dumped her squarely onto the hatches of the *Union Star*. For a moment all her keel was visible. Then the coaster rolled back, and the lifeboat twisted round and slid off, stern first, into the water.

The watchers in the helicopter and on the *Union Star* held their breath, not knowing what damage she had sustained, waiting to see if she could still float or whether she would go on sliding down to founder under the next wave. A moment passed, and then the watchers saw to their astonishment that the lifeboat was not only still afloat, but still under control and still, incredibly, closing once more towards the rail of the larger vessel.

Buckfield was hurtling down Tregiffian Lane with Harry Pender of Mousehole Cliff Rescue Team. Near the bottom he drove through a pool of floodwater and almost at once the Land Rover's engine coughed and died (due to a cracked distributor cap as it later turned out). Almost weeping with frustration he tried time and again to restart the engine. Then he saw lights coming up the lane towards him.

Pezzack had seen the *Union Star* go abeam, but as they entered the breakers, both vessels disappeared from his view under the edge of the cliff. He had been on the scene for forty minutes without any sign of official help arriving, and he was now rushing off to see if it was on its way. He saw Buckfield's flashing lamp and went to meet him. The Land Rover still declined to start and so they transferred the equipment to Pezzack's van and went back down the lane.

In Dartford, Kent, William Henry Rayner, a senior director of Union Transport, received a phone call at his aunt's house. He was not on duty, but the duty officer had managed to trace him. Bad news was coming in from Cornwall. It seemed that the *Union Star* was in distress, and a rescue operation was under way. There were no further details. Rayner tried to contact Falmouth Coastguards, but for some time he was unable to get through.

From the *Noord Holland*, about a mile out it was hard to see exactly how close the *Union Star* was to the cliffs. However, when he saw her lights change as she turned sideways, Buurman could not keep silent, and called out a warning to the lifeboat. The Penlee radio operator was understandably out of breath, but found time to acknowledge the warning.

The sight of the *Solomon Browne* crashing onto their decks right before their eyes finally galvanised the *Union Star's* crew. They could see the edge of the cliff, where the breakers were throwing spray 30 metres (100ft) into the air. The lifeboat was their last hope, and it had almost been smashed to pieces in front of them. Time had run out.

Suddenly the wheelhouse door opened and the passengers, clad in orange lifejackets, rushed out onto the terrible decks. They fled to the port side, down the ladder and onto the side decks. As they reached the rail, a mountain of freezing black water rushed out of the shadows, burst over the ship's side and buried them.

The *Union Star* rolled with the blow and her side lifted high in the air. As she righted herself, thousands of gallons poured back off the hatches, pinning the survivors to the rail, trying to drag them through. Slowly the water cleared for a brief respite.

And there was the *Solomon Browne*.

By a marvellous piece of seamanship, Trevelyan had timed her approach so that she came alongside in a brief moment of choppy confusion between major seas. The lifeboat sliced through the few metres of foam and crashed against the coaster's side. At last the willing

THE UNBLEMISHED HULL OF THE *UNION STAR* STILL POUNDED BY HEAVY SEAS ON THE MORNING OF 20TH DECEMBER 1981.

THE UPTURNED *UNION STAR* AT DAWN ON 20TH DECEMBER 1981. IT IS SWEPT BY WAVES THAT HAVE MODERATED CONSIDERIBLY SINCE THE STORMY NIGHT BUT THEIR MAGNITUDE CAN BE GAUGED BY COMPARISON WITH THE WRECK WHICH IS 67 METRES (220FT) LONG.

hands of the crew, who had reached out in vain for so long, had work to do. They hauled across as many survivors as they could reach with desperate haste, and packed them inside the cabin. As late as he dared, Trevelyan broke contact and headed out to sea.

But they hadn't all made it.

As they parted, at least one orange lifejacket was in the water, probably two. Two more were still visible, clinging to the rail as the next wave engulfed them again. They were 45 metres (50 yds) from shore, and in amongst the breakers. All around them the sea was tearing itself apart.

It was nine twenty-one.

21.21

<u>Penlee Lifeboat to Falmouth Coastguard:</u> Falmouth Coastguard, this is the Penlee Lifeboat, Penlee Lifeboat calling Falmouth Coastguard.
<u>Falmouth Coastguard to Penlee Lifeboat:</u> Falmouth Coastguard, Penlee Lifeboat, go.
<u>Penlee Lifeboat to Falmouth Coastguard:</u> We got four men off - look er hang on - we got four off at the moment er mai - male and female. There's two left on board …

There was a crashing noise, and the message ended abruptly.

But the *Solomon Browne* still lived. Both Buurman and the helicopter crew saw her clearly after the last communication. Russell Smith, shocked but relieved that at least some lives had been saved at the very end, gratefully hauled the Sea King up to safer height. He had been flying under extreme stress for two and a half hours, and now gladly eased his aircraft out of the trap which had so nearly caught her. Without even waiting to see what became of the *Union Star* - now rolling in the breakers and almost ashore - he throttled forward and headed for home, passing over the *Noord Holland* on the way. When he last saw the *Solomon Browne* she was upright and heading to seaward.

The *Solomon Browne* was left alone. Buttery and Hoare were struggling around Tater Du to the east, Townsend was ascending Carn Boscawen to the west, and above, Buckfield, Pender and Pezzack were just returning in Pezzack's van. Unbelievably, no one was watching at all.

"There's two left on board…"

Guy Buurman suddenly saw the lifeboat high in the air on a crest, silhouetted by the coaster's lights. A moment later the *Union Star's* lights disappeared as her long drift finally came to an end. Her starboard side snagged a reef, and a giant wall of water tipped her over like a child's toy and threw her upside down onto the granite shore.

Above, the smell of diesel suddenly mingled with the rain and spray.

EIGHT

21.22
<u>Falmouth Coastguard to Penlee Lifeboat</u>: Penlee Lifeboat Falmouth Coastguard - I understand you have four off and you say there's two left on board over.

21.23
<u>Falmouth Coastguard to Penlee Lifeboat</u>: Penlee Lifeboat Penlee Lifeboat Falmouth Coastguard over.

21.24
<u>Falmouth Coastguard to Penlee Lifeboat</u>: Penlee Lifeboat Penlee Lifeboat Falmouth Coastguard over.

21.27
<u>Falmouth Coastguard to Penlee Lifeboat</u>: Penlee Lifeboat Penlee Lifeboat Falmouth Coastguard over.

21.28
<u>Noord Holland to Penlee Lifeboat</u>: Newlyn Lifeboat er Newlyn Lifeboat Noord Holland.

21.31
<u>Falmouth Coastguard to Penlee Lifeboat</u>: Penlee Lifeboat Penlee Lifeboat Falmouth Coastguard over.

21.33
<u>Rescue 80 to Penlee Lifeboat</u>: Penlee Lifeboat this is Rescue Eight Zero.

21.33
<u>Rescue 80 to Falmouth Coastguard</u>: Falmouth Coastguard this is Rescue Eight Zero, I am not receiving Penlee Lifeboat either.

21.41
<u>Falmouth Coastguard to Noord Holland</u>: Tug Noord Holland Falmouth Coastguard are you in touch with Penlee Lifeboat over?

21.41
<u>Noord Holland to Falmouth Coastguard</u>: No we're listening out on sixteen but I think the people are very busy so I don't want to interfere over.

21.45
<u>Falmouth Coastguard to Noord Holland</u>: Noord Holland Falmouth Coastguard can you confirm have you got the lifeboat visual still over?

21.45
<u>Noord Holland to Falmouth Coastguard</u>: Er the lifeboat is very close to the shore and I see a lot of searchlights on the coast - it's very dark - er it's still force ten-eleven with high seas ... we just wait one mile out of the coast and er we are also wondering what happened.

NINE

———————

Pezzack arrived back at the bottom of the lane with Buckfield and Pender and they all jumped out and peered seawards. Apart from the distant *Noord Holland* the sea was quite empty. The smell of diesel was overwhelming. Pezzack led the way along the path and down a side track to a small point, bent double, as they all were to make headway into the wind. They reached the edge and looked over.

Buckfield stared down at 'Echo A'. Her huge smooth hull, without a blemish upon it, was turned up to the sky, the rudder sticking up high in the air. Waves crashed over it. She was lying at the end of the point, with one side of the bridge turned towards them. The emergency lighting had stayed on, illuminating a doorway and porthole in the wheelhouse. The rope ladder thrown out by the crewman was still attached.

Pezzack thought he could see a red light further away across the cove, but he could not be sure. Buckfield went back to organise the other Cliff Rescue Teams from Sennen and Treen who were now arriving. At last lanterns and floodlights began to shine out, and equipment was carried down to the point. As Buckfield was talking to one of the Sennen crew, they both saw what looked like a figure jumping from the *Union Star's* wheelhouse door into the sea. This added urgency to the situation, and Buckfield instructed his team to lower him over the edge at once.

It was an arduous and dangerous business. The wind tossed him like a shuttlecock, and he was assaulted by a foul mixture of spray, diesel and fertiliser which struck him in the face at up to 160kmph (100mph). As he descended further he was surprised to find conditions becoming slightly easier. The *Union Star* itself was lending him a lee, its bulk providing him with a little protection.

Shining his torch around he could see plenty of flotsam and small items of wreckage, but no sign of any survivors. Not that he had expected any. Looking out to sea, he could see waves breaking metres offshore but not diminishing in height as they rushed in, somehow remaining about 9 metres (30ft) high until they hit the rocks. A ledge was breaking water about a hundred 91 metres (100 yds) out. It was impossible to imagine anyone surviving for more than a few seconds in such water.

Looking around, Buckfield saw a deep gully in the cliff - a 'zawn' as they are known locally - behind the *Union Star's* stern. It was the innermost point of the shallow bay and the natural place for floating objects to collect. A light was shining in the surf.

He quickly gave the signal to be hauled up, and had the rescue equipment moved to the side of the zawn. As soon as it was ready he went over again.

The zawn was deep and sheer, and it was a long time before he could touch his feet onto anything solid. Waves were rushing up the opening, losing themselves amongst the rounded boulders. The zawn was already filled with wreckage, most of it unrecognisable.

He spotted the light at once. It was attached to a red lifejacket which was moving to and fro in the breakers. He made every effort to get hold of it, trying to time a run between the waves, but it stubbornly eluded him. He wanted it for corroboration, but he had few doubts about what it was. Buckfield had seen standard-issue RNLI lifejackets often enough. Sick with apprehension he was hauled up to the cliff-top once again.

Having mustered at the *Union Star*, there was now not a great deal for the Cliff Rescue Team to do. There seemed to be no survivors to rescue, and trying to board the wreck was out of the question until the storm moderated and the tide fell. Buckfield set up headquarters in a barn at the farm, made sure there was an illuminated way down to the rocks, and checked out a suitable field for helicopter operations at daybreak. He sent out teams of twos and threes on the dangerous mission of searching along the coastline to the east and west. Judging by the set of the weather, he reckoned that anything not found between Boscawen and Tater Du would be driven into the deeper cove of Lamorna. He agreed that Martin Tregoning, the Land's End station officer, should take a crew and equipment back to the cove and keep a look-out there. There was little else he could do, but hope for the best. Many of the *Solomon Browne's* crew were personal friends. Where was she? He could only listen and wait.

Others were listening and waiting. The R80's crew were listening at Culdrose, tired, depressed and overawed at what they had seen. They were having a rest and refreshment, ready to return if necessary.

Buurman listened, continuing his lonely patrol, coming in closer as the tide swelled. He was in no small danger himself in the very eye of the storm, fully occupied in coping with the waves.

Captain Ian Cooke listened in St Ives Bay aboard the *Union Jupiter*, knowing his sister ship was lost but unaware how many of his friends were dead. All the other sheltering boats listened too - Channel 16 had been cleared of all other traffic except that relating to the emergency.

Rayner waited by the telephone in Kent. He had gone home as soon as the Coastguards told him the *Union Star* was ashore. They told him the lifeboat had rescued four of the crew. Rayner still knew nothing of Dawn, Sharon or Deanne, and took some comfort from the fact that only one crewman seemed to be missing, though he did not know who.

In Newlyn and Mousehole they listened hardest of all. Many fishing families had radio sets at home and had followed the whole crisis. A number of skippers were in Newlyn already checking their moorings as the wind tore into the harbour. As the lifeboat's silence became deafening, they thought they might be able to contact her more easily than Falmouth, especially if she was on reduced power for some reason. A chorus of concern arose over the airwaves.

"Can you hear us, Trev?"
"What is your position?"
"Do you need any help?"
"Shall we come out, Trev?"

Then at about quarter past ten, the clouds seemed to lift. The Auxiliary Coastguard at Penzer Point to the west of Mousehole reported lights below, heading into the bay.

The timing was right for the lifeboat. The usual rescue procedure was for her to put into Newlyn, when injured casualties would be taken away by ambulance, and those who needed only shelter and comfort would be taken to the 'Mission' - the Royal National Mission for Deep Sea Fishermen - which acts as a hostelry for all sailors in distress. The ambulance and police were duly called, and the Mission was opened up in readiness. A few people gathered to welcome the lifeboat in, and strained their eyes into the gale to see her lights coming round the point.

It is only a ten-minute journey from Penzer Point to Newlyn. After half an hour or so it became cruelly obvious that she wasn't coming. The reception committee broke up in distress, starting to put into words what they could hardly bear to think.

But the rest of the now thoroughly-awakened news media were still putting out the story that the lifeboat had rescued four and had been seen returning home. Around the area anxious people relaxed and went back to their Saturday-night amusements.

The lights at Penzer Point remain a mystery.

THE *VINCENT NESFIELD*, THE 'ROTHER' CLASS LIFEBOAT STATIONED AT SENNEN COVE.

TEN

Mike Sutherland, the Penzance and Newlyn pilot, was on standby at home when he received a call from Falmouth Coastguards. They said Penlee had done "a damn fine job" and was returning to Newlyn with four survivors. Shortly afterwards he had a call from Dudley Penrose, the Penlee launcher, whose tone was quite different. Penrose knew the coast as well as any, and was sick with worry. Sutherland went to the Newlyn pilot boat and called on the radio for half an hour. Then he took a mobile radio and, picking up Penrose on the way, went out in the car and on foot, keeping as close to the sea as possible, calling and listening on the mobile. Overhead they could head the sound of an aircraft. R80 was back.

The helicopter crew were expecting to be recalled as the lack of news went on. When they had last seen the lifeboat she had seemed to be heading for safety, but anything might have happened. The Sea King took off with trepidation, for high winds can cause 'blade-sailing' - an unfortunate tendency of the main rotor blades to wag up and down as they start to turn, sometimes so much that they hit the ground and shatter. Once in the air the flying conditions were described by the normally unemotional Smith as "horrific". The helicopter's maximum speed was about 120 knots, but even then some of the gusts stopped her in the air. Accurate search patterns were impossible. She was well outside her official tolerances for wind-speed and turbulence.

Nevertheless search she did, for over an hour, up and down the coast. When they could find no trace of the lifeboat, the crew tried one last avenue.

"Penlee Lifeboat, Rescue Eight Zero, if you read me fire a flare"
... if you read me fire a flare"
... fire a flare"

The plaintive message was repeated and repeated, but the skies remained dark. There seemed no point in risking their lives any longer, and R80 flew sadly back to Culdrose. Smith, Docherty, Kennie and Marlow stood down, and a fresh crew prepared to commence a thorough search at first light.

Sutherland and Penrose went back to Penrose's house, had a cup of tea and waited. Their mood was grim, knowing that little hope remained. Nevertheless Sutherland felt that someone should take a look at sea level. His thoughts turned to his flank RNLI stations, i.e. Sennen and the Lizard/Cadgwith.

Neither was an easy option. The Lizard would have to beat across miles of open bay, while Sennen would launch into sheltered waters but would meet the wind and waves head-on at Land's End. Sutherland rang the honorary secretary of the Sennen lifeboat, who told him that the coxswain was already in the boathouse preparing to launch.

For a multiple launching of lifeboats, RNLI regulations require clearance and co-ordination from their headquarters in Poole. Both Sutherland and the Coastguards had given Poole a complete update. Sutherland himself contacted The Lizard lifeboat; and Poole - not liking the prospects of either of the nearest flank stations -rang through to St Mary's in the Isles of Scilly and asked them if they would be prepared to go out. The answer of course was yes.

THE *DUKE OF CORNWALL*, THE LIZARD/CADGWITH LIFEBOAT OF THE 'BARNET' CLASS, VERY SIMILAR TO THE *SOLOMON BROWNE*.

MATT LETHBRIDGE, COXSWAIN OF THE ISLES OF SCILLY LIFEBOAT, THE *ROBERT EDGAR*.

Maurice Hutchens, coxswain of the Sennen lifeboat had been at home, finishing off some decorating. He heard reports of Penlee's operation on his radio scanner, but was not unduly alarmed. Sennen is often the least sheltered of villages, but the southerly gale was passing by overhead and the village was relatively quiet. He went out for a drink with his wife to Land's End, and when he saw the true state of conditions he quickly returned home. They were still calling for Penlee on the radio. He went straight to his boathouse and started trying to assemble a crew. Most of the regulars were out for the evening. Eventually he managed to collect four other volunteers.

Sennen had an 'Rother' class relief lifeboat the *Vincent Nesfield*, only 11.2 metres (37ft) long, and it was supposed to have a crew of seven in bad weather. However no one else was available.

None of them were under much illusion as to their chances of even reaching the southern coast. Sennen cove was relatively calm, but in a mile or two they would have to pass the bastion of Land's End and meet the weather full in the face. Land's End is a notorious passage in any weather, where two tides meet in an area of confused water. The tide was now all wrong, running down towards the weather. In such conditions the waves tend to rise up almost vertically, curl over and collapse in on themselves, and woe betide any boat caught beneath. After some dispute, they agreed that they should at least go out and see if it was possible to get around. If it proved futile, at least they would have tried.

Peter Mitchell, coxswain of the Lizard/ Cadgwith lifeboat, had an evening remarkably similar to Hutchens. Aware of the emergency, he had gone to the pub when the news of Penlee's 'sighting' was reported, but he also returned uneasily after a single pint. He waited at home for the call he was expecting.

When it came, he went down with difficulty to the lifeboat house, for a tree had blown across the lane. As he and several helpers hauled it out of the way he saw the maroons go up - the rockets were whipped half a mile downwind before exploding. He arrived with a full crew and runners at the boathouse, and the *Duke of Cornwall* was prepared for launching. She was a 'Barnet' class - of a very similar age and type as the *Solomon Browne*, but a little longer. Mitchell had no illusions about his prospects either. The wind was working round slightly towards the south-west, and he had nearly twenty miles of open water to cross into the very teeth of it.

When Matt Lethbridge's call came in the Scilly Isles, he had assumed that Penlee was already safely back in Newlyn. "God isn't she back yet?" he exclaimed. He was asked to stand by, and called the crew to his house to save time.

Hugh Town harbour on St Mary's is dominated by the square shape and long slipway of the lifeboat station, but their old Watson would not be splashing down the slipway tonight. Instead the recently acquired 17,38 metres (52ft) 'Arun' class *Robert Edgar* was riding at her moorings in the harbour, one of the first of the radical new design of fast upright-style lifeboats to be deployed. She had not yet been out on a really dirty night, and it promised to be a new experience at least. The call soon came, and Lethbridge and his crew also set off for their boat.

Saturday the nineteenth of December had turned into Sunday the twentieth. On the radio - for the first time that night - Mayday was being broadcast, listing the Penlee lifeboat as "overdue".

With few illusions as to the fate of their comrades, twenty-one more men detached themselves from the warmth and safety of their homes, and cast themselves into hazard, entrusting themselves as the mood took them to experience, luck and the Almighty.

One after another the three lifeboats put to sea.

THE *ROBERT EDGAR*, THE ISLES OF SCILLY LIFEBOAT, THEN NEW, ONE OF THE FAST UPRIGHT–STYLE BOATS.

ELEVEN

Some of the coastal parties radiating from Tater Du had arrived back at Lamorna to find quantities of wreckage in the bay, starting to come ashore. When Tregoning arrived, he saw a growing line of weed and flotsam forming over the round granite boulders, and amongst it larger pieces of wreckage. There was more in the surf; lengths of broken timber, air-boxes, a blanket, clothing and other, grimmer evidence. One glance told the whole story - lifeboats have a highly distinctive livery and specialised equipment, and there were pieces of it everywhere.

Avoiding the open channel, Tregoning reported his finds. Other assistance was sent to him. Mike Sutherland and Dudley Penrose went straight to Lamorna. When they arrived the police were sealing off the cove. The CRE crews and helpers were pulling wreckage whenever they could reach it and laying it on the car park. It was a highly dangerous procedure, stumbling amongst the boulders in the darkness and rain, constantly threatened by the huge seas. Waves breaking over the harbour wall threw pieces of wreckage onto the car park. The normally placid cove was a scene from a nightmare.

One look was enough for Sutherland, and he went up the valley to the pub 'The Wink' to use the telephone. He managed to contact the Penlee honorary secretary Del Johnson, who had come home from his Saturday evening out to find the world falling about his ears. They arranged to rendezvous and start attending to the hundreds of details the new situation demanded. Their lifeboat was gone, but there was no time yet to mourn.

As many of the Penlee committee as could be contacted met in the harbour-master's office in Newlyn. Their priority was the families - a disparate group of eight households, now welded together by the chance demands of a night's lifeboat service. They wanted to carry the news to them before they heard it through another source. They had three GPs available, including Dr Leslie, and split into three parties, one representative of Penlee and one doctor each, allocating the families between them.

Rumours of the lifeboat wreckage were already circulating around Mousehole. The families and friends of the crew were in a high state of nerves - there was always hope, but by now they were dreading the worst. However, it was one thing to dread the worst and quite an.other to have it confirmed on your doorstep by a grim-faced friend with a doctor in attendance. "Some took it very quietly," said one of those entrusted with the awful task, "others not so".

After that, the news was broadcast to the rescue services, the media and the world at large.

The media were not slow to respond. The wreck of the coaster was a solid and worthwhile piece of news, but the wreck of a lifeboat also, in heroic circumstances - all the crew from one picturesque and well-known village - elevated it to the highest category. Front-line journalists and TV crews were shaken out of bed and pointed westwards in numbers.

Preliminary enquiries revealed that there had been some disagreement about accepting a tow, involving international negotiations, while time slipped away. This added a whiff of scandal, which raised the story again from the tragic to the controversial. There was room for opinion as well as sympathy. It drove all other news into the shadows, and the word 'Penlee' emerged from its local obscurity to become a media by-word. The news spread around the country, and rapidly across the English-speaking world. Before morning, although they little knew or cared, the families were already world-famous, and Mousehole was exposed to the well-meaning but merciless glare of the international media.

In the village the streets were full of shocked human traffic, going from house to house all night, visiting each other, weeping, talking or remaining silent, making tea, lending each other what support they could, unable to comprehend the tragedy that had befallen them. The eight men were all big personalities, confident, exuberant, involved in every strand of village life. To lose any one of them would have caused the whole village to grieve. To lose them all was a numbing wound, too deep for pain, too dreadful to grasp.

The streets of the village became busier and busier as the night wore away, but most of West Cornwall slept on unaware.

There was no time for sleep or mourning on the lifeboats still at sea.

Hutchens had gone down the short distance to Land's End. Like the other coxswains, he found the night exceptionally dark, with no visibility at all around their own small island of light. In some ways it was merciful, since the eye could not measure the size of the oncoming waves, and there was no time to fear. As they came close to the point, where the tide was 'leaning' against the weather, the *Vincent Nesfield* started climbing a vertical wall of water in the darkness. It reminded Hutchens not so much of the side of a house as the side of the church tower. Once was enough. He crested the wave, dropped into the trough and turned straight back. To pass Land's End in this weather would have meant a detour almost as far as the Wolf Rock. His intention was to wait around until the tide and weather were more favourable, but as more reports came over the radio, there seemed to be less and less point. The *Vincent Nesfield* turned disconsolately for home.

Lethbridge made sure all his crew were strapped into their seats as they left the islands on the *Robert Edgar*. They were taking the weather on the starboard bow and this created a strange slewing motion, speeding along, sometimes upright and sometimes virtually on their side. Their Decca navigator had packed up just as they hit the weather, and they had to slow down to take bearings from the Wolf Rock lighthouse, but apart from that they never paused in their headlong rush through the darkness. They surfed - or so legend has it - for quarter of a mile on a single wave. Their speed almost led to their undoing As they neared the mainland they saw the light of the Runnelstone Buoy, but as they closed on it they suddenly saw a red port light as well and realised that their 'buoy' was in fact another vessel. There was no time for avoiding action, and they passed it by, whatever it was, (possibly the *Noord Holland*) with very little room to spare. Shortly afterwards they slowed down and began to search. They had made the crossing in barely two hours.

The *Duke of Cornwall* had the worst of it. Mitchell too could see nothing ahead, not even the waves. Occasionally a line of foam caught the light, high above his masthead. They were travelling at their full speed of nine knots, ploughing into the rising waves, tipping upwards and over, and then falling over into the next trough as if falling off a cliff. Down they went, 9-12 metres (30-40ft), until the floor of the trough brought them up short with a sudden shocking impact. This went on for mile after mile, and hour after hour. The crew had nothing to do but endure the jarring blows, seasickness, and constant threat of injuries They were all afraid - even a lifeboat is not designed to take punishment on that scale indefinitely.

At last, at about 03.00 the *Duke of Cornwall* also arrived at the search area, and joined the *Robert Edgar* in her task. Shortly after they arrived the *Duke of Cornwall* tumbled so suddenly into a deep trough that three of the men who were forward were, as Mitchell said, "virtually left in mid-air". They fell heavily onto the deck, slipping towards the water, but one of them managed to hang on, and they all clung together. After about an hour and a half, the *Duke of Cornwall* put into Newlyn for a rest. The urgency had gone from the situation, and they were battered, tired and hungry. It was not until he disembarked that Mitchell even noticed his ship's rail. It had been beaten flat on the port side by waves alone.

There was already a TV crew on the quay as they went into the Mission. When they came out, the wind had almost gone. The waves were still huge, but the fury of the storm had passed, even more suddenly than it had come. They put to sea once more, to rejoin the *Robert Edgar* and work the day through.

A HELICOPTER SWEEPS THE STILL DISTURBED WATERS OF THE BAY BY ST MICHAEL'S MOUNT.

TWELVE

A ll nights eventually come to an end. A grey light filtered through the darkness at about eight o'clock, barely twelve hours since the lifeboatmen had left their homes.

It being a Sunday, people woke and rose at a more relaxed pace, and were not as quick to switch on their radios as usual. So the news spread gradually, often by telephone or word of mouth. Even for those who were not friends or family of the crew, it struck with a hurt which was both deep and personal. The normally quiet streets were full of people, walking without speaking. Others visited each other and sat together, unable to think or speak about anything else.

The pain spread far beyond the county. Cornwall has a special place in the affections of many people, and the telephone lines were constantly busy with exiled families, friends, holidaymakers, and other well wishers. Many more sat down to pour out their hearts in letters.

A Sea King helicopter arrived at Tregiffian at dawn, and at once commenced a search. Others followed, searching all day and for several thereafter. The coast parties continued all day also, constantly sweeping up and down the coast from Tater Du to Penzance. At sea a small flotilla of fishing boats joined the *Robert Edgar* and *Duke of Cornwall*. The seas were still dangerously high, but the fishermen were too upset to care, and succeeded in recovering a great deal of wreckage. Mike Sutherland took out the Newlyn pilot boat from the moorings where he and Stephen Madron had secured her the night before, and went out into the bay to look for Stephen. He failed to find him, but like many others found a private place out at sea to express his grief. When he returned the quay was thronged with newsmen.

A team of Royal Navy divers had arrived at Tregiffian during the night and had actually succeeded in reaching the *Union Star* but were unable to get in. At dawn a 'Bomb Bag' was flown in and a hole was blasted in the coaster's side. To the divers' consternation this set her on fire, and they had to extinguish this before they could enter. They finally managed to get in and make a thorough search. They found no one; but the accommodation was dry.

At Union Transport, Rayner was having the worst day of his life. The company did not have the luxury of a press officer, and had little experience of journalists. There was a lot of work to do regarding the disposal of the *Union Star*. But the press besieged them from early morning onwards, frightening in their persistence, and worst of all far better informed than anyone in the company. "Why were the women and children on board?" - "Why had the *Union Star* made an unauthorised stop?" - "Why had they refused to accept a tow?" - "Was it a row about the money?"

And so it went on. Each time the telephone rang Rayner discovered more circumstances he had been unaware of. Eventually he scheduled a press conference for later in the day.

It turned out to be a tense farce. Rayner was legally advised to stonewall and "no comment" anything the company wasn't sure of, which was nearly everything. This had the effect of making the company look uncaring and shifty. The press were armed with the fact that the Union Star was foreign-registered, and with Moreton's unfortunate remark about the tug and the money, they went to town. The blame for the Penlee disaster was laid squarely at the door of Union Transport and Mick Moreton, and there was no appeal.

At last the press dispersed, and Rayner was able to get on with his principal task of the day. It was to contact, comfort, and where necessary make provision for Bridie Moreton in Kent who had lost not only her beloved son but also his lively new family; Brenda Sedgwick in Hull with her three children, two still at school; Eileen Whittaker in Kent, married and widowed in the same year; Agostinho Verressimo's brother in Rotterdam; and Manuel Lopez's mother Cinda, who lived in Italy.

In Mousehole the streets were thronged with people, young and old, nearly all of them in tears. They gathered together in groups, close together but often not speaking. The Christmas lights and displays swung in the wind. John Blewett had organised their electrics, most of the crew had helped to put them up, and Charlie Greenhaugh had switched them on the night before last. And now helicopters were sweeping up and down the bay in front of the village, searching for their bodies. It was unreal.

Del Johnson, the Penlee honorary secretary, worked for Penzance shipping agents J H Bennetts, and they dedicated offices, telephones and a teleprinter to cope with the flood of callers. Volunteers were drafted in to help. The first telegrams to arrive came from other RNLI stations, who knew whom to contact. They knew more than most what it felt like, and poignant messages arrived from Longhope and Fraserburgh amongst many others. Messages of sympathy arrived from shipping companies - always aware of how much they owed the RNLI - maritime officials, MPs, the Prime Minister, and the Queen. Journalists were on the phone and at the door. There were a thousand things to organise.

An ad hoc visit to Mousehole by Johnson and other Penlee officers was met by ex-lifeboatmen and launching crew. What if there was another emergency? How soon could they have a relief lifeboat? They could easily find a crew for it - two if Del needed it. Neil Brockman was amongst the first volunteers. They were all adamant - you couldn't have a lifeboat station without a lifeboat. They might be needed again at any time. Johnson promised to do what he could.

The search for the dead continued on foot, by sea and by air. It was not in vain. Trevelyan was one of the first to be found, floating quietly in the sea between Tater Du and Lamorna, where he had fished all his life. In the same area the helicopters picked up Manuel Lopez and young Sharon Brown. Charlie Greenhaugh was found in Lamorna Cove, and George Sedgwick off Penzance promenade. The roads which skirted the bay were closed to all but essential traffic.

The wind dropped right away and the sun came out. It was a beautiful afternoon.

The Robert Edgar came in at tea-time for food and fuel. While in Newlyn, Lethbridge discovered that spray had come into the engine room through the air-intakes, and a fine layer of salt had encrusted the whole engine. Fortunately no damage had been done, and they washed it off with soapy water. After tea, they followed a call to St Michael's Mount and found the stern section of the Solomon Browne. After towing it back into Newlyn, they were at last stood down and were able to set course back to the islands and home. They arrived back at St Mary's at about nine in the evening.

Peter Mitchell was also relieved when advised that the *Duke of Cornwall* could turn her bows towards home. The sea was rolling, but glassy smooth. They arrived back after dark, and exhausted as he was Mitchell waited while his lifeboat was hauled back up the slipway. A lifeboat service is not complete until the boat is re-fuelled and ready for sea once more. As she rose out of the water, he noticed that she seemed to be dripping more water than usual. He had a look underneath, and was astonished at what he saw. The 'Barnet' had two bilge-keels - square lengths of timber bolted to the outside of the main hull for the vessel to rest on when not in the water - and the port keel had split down the middle for much of its length. The fixing bolts had worked loose, allowing water to enter around them. He opened the bungs. It took almost half an hour for her to drain. She had been full of water and, but for the airtight compartments and flotation boxes, she too would have foundered.

As darkness fell over the western peninsula, the first shock was turning to grief-stricken despair. The long Sunday went on and on.

THE WRECK OF THE *UNION STAR* IN CALMER WEATHER.

THIRTEEN

The week before Christmas passed like a bad dream. In the newspapers, Union Transport were savaged as a heartless multi-national which sent out badly crewed vessels under flags of convenience, and quibbled over salvage if they got into difficulties. These points were picked up and amplified in parliament by the MP representing the Seamen's Union, John Prescott. Despite refutations by themselves and by Weissmuller, the mud stuck, and the company could stop the general flow of abuse only by eventually issuing writs against six of the major newspapers.

The weather remained calm and peaceful. Dawn Moreton's body was discovered at Lamorna, and so too was Nigel Brockman's. The last body to be recovered, that of John Blewett, was not found until Boxing Day.

Penlee RNLI held a meeting of volunteers for the next lifeboat in the Mission in Newlyn. A relief lifeboat, the 21 metres (70ft) *Charles Henry Barrett*, had quietly slipped into Newlyn the night before. The basis of a new crew, a reserve crew and training schedule, etc. were discussed. The need to be an effective lifeboat station once more was urgent. It was the first step in alleviating the wound, and a way back to hope and self-respect. The press, who were still thronging the area, were excluded, and the volunteers refused to be photographed on leaving.

Another main centre of activity was the Penlee Relief Fund - or rather the funds. Public grief had expressed itself, as so often, with gifts of money. Twelve children had lost their fathers, and the whole country turned out their pockets to ensure that they, and indeed none of the families, should suffer want because of their menfolk's bravery. There was money everywhere, arriving by letter, by hand, in cheques, in cash, in bags and buckets. An official fund was quickly set up by the chairman of Penwith District Council, Arthur Berryman, with donations directed to Barclays Bank in Penzance. There the staff and volunteers worked for hour after hour to keep up with the flow. The trustees included a number of local dignitaries, as well as representatives from Penlee and Mousehole.

Despite the hard work and excellent intentions of the official fund's organisers, it was treated by a number of locals with some suspicion. No one had forgotten the miserable outcome of the Aberfan Disaster Appeal, where £1.25 million was collected, only to be tied up in legal arguments for years and eventually distributed amidst bitterness and acrimony. For Cornish people with long memories, the example of the Levant Mine disaster of 1919 was even closer to home. On that occasion a large disaster fund was administered by a committee of local grandees with admirable fiscal prudence but little regard to the dignity of the dependants, who had been forced to plead and prove their need every time they applied for assistance.

Cornish working people are as pragmatic as any and a second fund arose alongside the first, the 'Fisherman's Fund' in Newlyn. There money was collected, counted and accounted, split eight ways and taken directly to Mousehole for immediate distribution. Daphne Lawry, president of the Cornwall Fisherman's Association, was in charge, assisted by an army of willing helpers. Much of the local donation went to this source, while the 'up-country' money was arriving at the official fund.

Wednesday the twenty-third of December was in many ways the saddest day. It was Tom Bawcock's Eve, a strictly Mousehole celebration, commemorating a Mousehole fisherman who alone had ventured out one terrible winter to relieve the starving village, and had returned on twenty-third of December with his hold packed with 'seven different sorts of fish'. A celebration was held every year in the 'Ship', where Tom Bawcock was impersonated and a special fish pie was baked and distributed with much revelry and intemperance.

Twenty-third December 1981 saw Mousehole road-blocked to discourage sightseers, dark, deserted and forlorn. A scrap of paper in the 'Ship's' window read simply "Tom Bawcock's cancelled". In Nigel Brockman's house the black coat and bowler hat remain unused - he was to have been that year's Tom Bawcock. The village seemed buried in a sombre abyss.

A sign of hope was sorely needed, and it was provided. Some members of the Christmas lights committee had laboured quietly in the afternoon, and after dark the cross from the harbour wall shone out again in a new position, between the two kneeling angels on the hill, high above the village. Only these three pierced the darkness as a symbol of hope and faith.

Trevelyan Richards was buried at Paul on the morning of Christmas Eve, and Nigel Brockman in the same place in the afternoon. It was the first opportunity for open expression of grief and loss. The church was filled, and the services relayed outside. At times the emotion was almost too much to bear, but the services were concluded with dignity. Nigel Brockman's funeral ended with the hymn "Jesus Saviour Pilot Me" and the last stanza said everything:

"When at last I near the shore
And the fearful breakers roar
Twixt me and the peaceful rest
Then while leaning on Thy breast
May I hear Thee say to me
Fear not, I will pilot thee."

That evening, by request of the families, the lights were lit once more around the harbour. There were exceptions - the huge "MERRY CHRISTMAS" lay dark on the hill, as did the sea-serpent in the harbour, but for the eyes of the children and the hard work of the departed men the bright displays filled the village with colour, for an hour. Then the cross and angels resumed their vigil. In the houses, for the most part, even those who had until then made no gesture towards Christmas solemnly decorated their houses in the traditional way, and prepared to celebrate a quieter and more thoughtful Christmas than ever before. However sad and changed, life had to go on.

OPPOSITE: THE CROSS AND ANGELS SHINING ON THE HILL, HIGH ABOVE THE VILLAGE.

FOURTEEN

Soon after Christmas Jack Pender, the Mousehole representative of the Appeal Trustees, was given the uncomfortable task of going around to the families and explaining how the official fund would be administered. The trustees would need, he explained, details of their fuel bills, mortgage repayments, rates, electricity, etc. They were prevented, under the rules governing charities, from making any payments that would improve the standard of living of the families above that which they already enjoyed, or endured. The fund already stood at nearly two million pounds, and the question of how to distribute that between eight not particularly well-to-do working families without improving their standard of living had yet to be tackled. In fact it seemed likely that they would get nothing at all.

The forebodings which had led to the founding of the alternative fund seemed fully justified. It was Levant all over again.

A flame of anger blazed around the whole community when the news came out. There were threats of direct action, even of a march on London to see justice done.

There seemed to be no way out of the dilemma. If the fund was not administered under the charity regulations then it would have to be treated as a gift. As such it would come under the laws of taxation designed to prevent large gifts from rich people to their relatives, avoiding estate duty. Thus a vast amount of the money given in sorrow and sympathy in pubs, clubs and on the street, raised by sponsored walks, rides, rowing, football and rugby matches, special concerts, from official societies and humble individuals, - even a substantial sum donated by a whip-round from the ubiquitous journalists - would go whistling into the jaws of the taxman.

However even the taxman had little relish for such a windfall. The government, in the form of Attorney General, Sir Michael Havers, dropped a broad hint that something would be sorted out to try and accord with the wishes of the original donors. And so it was. When the Appeal Trustees went to London to meet the Charity Commissioners, together with representatives of the families and with Lord Goodman as their adviser, they found themselves knocking at an open door. The fund, it was decided could be classified as private, which avoided one horn of the dilemma; and the tax laws could be interpreted to refer to each donation individually not to the sum as a whole, which avoided the other. The families could have the money.

It was a hugely important psychological triumph, which did much to help the families and the future of the village as a community. The principle it established was that the money was given to the families as a tribute to their dead menfolk, in recognition of the way they had given their lives. The only fair way to distribute this was simply to divide it eight ways and pass it on. Later on when the fund grew to embarrassing proportions - £3 million was the final tally - it was the justice of this simple principle which prevented the worst excesses of bitterness and resentment which had dogged other similar funds. The money was all distributed and the Appeal Committee disbanded at the earliest opportunity.

The families expressed their gratitude, then did their best to withdraw from the public eye. There were a few more public occasions to face first. In late January the memorial service for the whole crew was held at Paul Church. All the other funerals had been held - including a particularly sad occasion at Lelant where Charlie Greenhaugh had been buried along with his mother, who had died two days after him of grief and shock. The thoughts of everyone at Paul were especially with those whose men the sea had taken and had not returned. The Mousehole Choir sang a setting of Tennyson's valedictory poem 'Crossing the Bar':

"Sunset and Evening Star
And one clear call for me…"

and once again emotion flowed in plenty. The service was attended by the Duke and Duchess of Kent. The Duchess in particular made a huge impression on everyone. She distributed inscribed silver crosses to all the next of kin. Mary Greenhaugh invited her to the 'Ship' for a drink, and she promised to come back when the fuss had died down - a promise she faithfully kept. And to remind them that they had been in Cornwall and not just anywhere, Mike Sutherland presented them with a couple of lobsters to take home, on behalf of Penlee RNLI.

Three weeks later a larger and more formal memorial service was held in Truro Cathedral. Mrs Thatcher and her husband attended in a private capacity, at the invitation of Kevin Smith's mother Pat, together with the Duke of Atholl, local and Euro MPs, and lords and ladies of the county. The lesson was from St John's Revelations:

"And God shall wipe away all tears from their eyes; and there shall be no more death; neither sorrow, nor crying; neither shall there be any more pain; for the former things are passed away."

It was movingly read in the strong Cornish tones of the Sennen coxswain, Maurice Hutchens. At the end, the band of the Royal Marines played "Sunset" and the flag of the RNLI was slowly lowered before the Cross on the High Altar.

In May the families appeared for the last time in public at the Royal Festival Hall at the special annual meeting of the RNLI. They received the medals posthumously awarded to the *Solomon Browne*'s crew - a gold medal for Trevelyan and bronze medals for the other seven. They stood bravely on the stage while the entire hall rose in spontaneous applause. And then at last they could go home and try to return to a normal life. Another medal - the Royal Humane Society's Silver Medal - was later awarded to Coastguard Don Buckfield.

The press moved on to other things, after a final flourish. The father of Sharon and Deanne Brown arrived in Penzance for Sharon's funeral. During his stay the somewhat flamboyant Mr Brown struck up a relationship with the barmaid in his hotel, and a whirlwind romance was followed by the announcement of their engagement. This was good copy, but when it emerged that Mr Brown already had a perfectly good wife back in Johannesburg, the papers could hardly contain their glee. With the addition of sex and scandal, the Penlee story had now had everything.

The RNLI also picked up the pieces. A permanent replacement boat arrived in the familiar shape of the *Guy and Clare Hunter*, which had been the Isles of Scilly lifeboat for many years. By mid February she was installed in the Penlee boathouse with a new coxswain - Ken Thomas from Newlyn - and a new crew, trained and ready for anything.

30 December 1981

Dear Commander Cooper,

On the night of Saturday, 19 December 1981, I was flying Sea King helicopter call sign "Rescue 80" during the rescue attempt on the Union Star. The courage and determination of the eight Penlee Lifeboatmen I believe should be mentioned lest other men forget or never know of their bravery.

About 20.45, the Penlee Lifeboat joined us to attempt the rescue of the five crewmen, a woman and two teenagers from the Union Star. The seas were 50 to 60 feet driven by hurricane force winds from the SWW. The Union Star's bow, midships and occasionally the bridge were awash in the violent and confused seas.

The Penlee Lifeboat made several successful attempts to come alongside the Union Star. The Lifeboat's crew were manning the rails and occasionally trying, unsuccessfully to get a man on board the Union Star. The Lifeboat was often bashed into the side of the Union Star before being washed or blown off. The Penlee was always deftly manoeuvred back alongside.

The Union Star eventually turned broadside in the breakers and the Penlee made another run-in. As the Penlee approached midship the Union Star, the Penlee was lifted by a wave and onto the hatch covers of the Union Star, then almost as quickly, slid off stern first into the sea. At this point people were seen running along the Union Star towards where the Penlee had just slid away. The Penlee quickly manoeuvred back alongside, picked up four people and steamed safely out from the Union Star about forty yards and just clear of the breakers. The Penlee broadcast she had four people on board and there were two left on the casualty. Subsequent to this the Penlee made a starboard turn.

Throughout the entire rescue evolution the Penlee crew never appeared to hesitate. After each time they were washed, blown or bumped away from the casualty the Penlee immediately commenced another run-in. Their spirit and dedication was amazing considering the horrific hurricane seas and the constant pounding they were taking. The greatest act of courage I have ever seen, and am likely to ever see, was the penultimate courage and dedication shown by the Penlee when it manoeuvred back alongside the casualty in over 60 foot breakers and rescuing four people shortly after the Penlee had been bashed on the top of the casualty's hatch covers.

They were truly the bravest eight men I've ever seen who were also totally dedicated to upholding the highest standards of the RNLI.

I most humbly submit this eyewitness account of professionalism, dedication and bravery to the RNLI with my deepest sympathy for the families of these great men.

Sincerely,

Russell L. Smith
Lt. Cdr. USN
Pilot of R.N. Sea King Helicopter
"Rescue 80"

Better days were coming for Penlee. Three days after the disaster, David Robinson, a retired millionaire and philanthropist who had already made substantial anonymous donations to the RNLI, pledged the necessary £450,000 for the building of a new 'Arun' class lifeboat to replace the *Solomon Browne*. The 'Arun' is not launched from a slipway, and so the Penlee lifeboat had to move back to moorings in Newlyn harbour, to within a short distance of where it had berthed in 1908. Mr Robinson wished the new vessel to be named after his wife, Mabel Alice. The 'Arun' had been ordered but would not be ready for another year. Meantime it was back to business as usual.

Only one matter remained unresolved. What had actually happened to the *Solomon Browne*? And whose fault was it?

THE *MABEL ALICE*, NAMED AFTER BENEFACTOR DAVID ROBINSON'S WIFE, BECAME PENLEE'S REPLACEMENT LIFEBOAT.

FIFTEEN

The inquest on the eight bodies recovered and the other eight "missing presumed drowned" was held in Penzance in March 1982. It was memorable for the letter sent by the helicopter pilot, Russell Smith, describing the last moments of the *Solomon Browne* and describing her crew as "the bravest eight men I have ever seen - totally dedicated to upholding the highest standards of the RNLI."

His evidence about the *Union Star* and its crew was less complimentary. He described how there seemed to be "little sense of urgency" on the part of the crew, how few efforts they made to co-operate with the helicopter, how a crewman "watched the lifeboat but made no attempt to get to it".

Other witnesses were equally damning. Buurman characterised Moreton as "short tempered". He said the *Union Star* had waited for an hour trying to find a Union Transport representative at home, but "everyone had been out".

Robbie Roberts, the Chief Coastguard, joined in, saying that Moreton had not considered himself in any danger.

The lesson was duly drawn by the Coroner's jury. Fifteen of the deaths were classified one by one as "accidental". When Moreton's was read out it was "misadventure" which, as the Coroner helpfully pointed out, was appropriate when someone had placed himself deliberately or unnecessarily in a position of peril.

The media's relationship with Union Transport was at rock bottom, and they happily seized upon the results of the inquest. A particularly unkind article described the fifty-year old engineer George Sedgwick as a "novice" - inspired by the fact that his latest papers were still being processed and had not caught up with him when he died. Considering the heroic way in which Sedgwick had spent his last hours, struggling for the *Union Star's* life, it was a cheap slur indeed.

Union Transport's lawsuit against the press was not settled until 1985, when the six newspapers agreed to pay damages of £30,000 with an apology in court. Union Transport immediately contributed this to the almost unknown '*Union Star* Appeal Fund' which then stood at £15,000 - most of which Union Transport had already contributed themselves. The £45,000 was distributed amongst the five *Union Star* families. It was all they ever got.

Nearly twelve months exactly after the inquest, on 14th March 1983, the long awaited formal investigation began its first day's work.

It was held in the Queen's Hotel on Penzance seafront. From the large picture windows Penlee Point and the angular boathouse drew the eye on many occasions.

Among the parties represented were Union Transport, the RNLI, the Irish Department of Transport (to quash any further attempts to denigrate the Irish Republic as a 'flag of convenience'), and HM Coastguard. The tally was made up by the slightly larger-than-life figure of Noel Horner, a Truro solicitor and ex-neighbour of Kevin Smith's, who had been retained by the Smith and Wallis families to make sure there was no whitewash.

Gerald Dorling QC opened the proceedings on behalf of the Department of Trade, and dismayed the Penlee families by opining - on Day I - that no one would be found to blame. They had thought that such a conclusion was the point of the enquiry, and should at least wait until the end. Horner went on the offensive and alleged fault against Moreton and two of the Coastguard officers. The battle lines were drawn. Without Horner the enquiry would probably have ended after a few days with everyone praising the lifeboatmen and blaming the weather. Horner was having none of this. He waded into the evidence and witnesses with relish. The assembled gentlemen, many of whom shared a common background in the Royal Navy, winced occasionally, and seemed fascinated by him.

To lay the burden of blame for such an unhappy and keenly felt tragedy on to the shoulders of any individual or group would have required incontrovertible evidence of negligence. Despite Homer's efforts, such evidence simply did not exist. In the end he was forced to withdraw his allegations.

The enquiry was diligent, thorough in its preparation and research, and truthful in its conclusions. Nevertheless it clearly saw its role as an emollient, a dispeller of rumour and controversy, and where the facts allowed interpretation, the interpretation chosen was always the least contentious.

This was well illustrated by the conclusions drawn from the disposal of the wreckage. A team of divers had investigated this, and one fine spring day a fresh ripple of shock ran round the community as the major portion of the lifeboat's keel, including the engines, was winched clear of the water. A rope was wound round the one surviving propeller in a tight embrace. The wreckage was about 274 metres (300 yds) to the east of the wreck of the Union Star.

It was a possible hypothesis that the lifeboat had fouled the rope in the confusion and, thus disabled, had been driven onto the rocks where she was found. However, the enquiry was treating the loss of the two vessels as a single incident. If the lifeboat had been lost in a separate incident of a different cause, it opened up a whole new and unwelcome line of questioning. The enquiry found that the lifeboat had been struck by the Union Star in her final moments, partly broken up, and had floated to the eastwards where she was driven ashore. The rope around her propeller was said to be 'similar' to the heavy mooring ropes used to link the two vessels together, accidentally discarded. It was said to have wound around the propeller as the shaft was "distracted by impact" However a number of local people identified the rope as the sea anchor rope, without much doubt picked up under way while going astern.

Another example concerned the entry of water into the Union Star's fuel tanks. An unreplaced or improperly fastened screw-cap was an obvious possibility. However, this would have involved responsibility, whereas a malfunctioning valve did not. A large amount of time and trouble was expended on experiments on 'Pres-Vac' valves to show that they could allow a constant flow of water under certain conditions, but the conditions were far from clear.

Everyone naturally fought his own corner. The coastguards, sensitive to the charge that the lifeboat had been launched too late, put great emphasis on the prerogative of the captain in a distress situation. They also laid stress on their apprehension that the lifeboatmen would - on being put on the previously little known "anticipatory" status - be in the boathouse ready to launch. Literally days were spent belabouring this point, although it would have made no more than 10-15 minutes difference. Far less stress was laid on the previous fifty minutes between the discovery of the polluted fuel and the order to launch. Of the thirty-five minutes between the order to scramble the already alerted helicopter and its actually taking the air, no mention was made at all.

George Thomas QC made a spirited defence of Moreton and Union Transport. With a speech that reflected the anger and frustration the company had borne in silence for fifteen months, he went through Moreton's choices and actions one by one. He managed to justify all of them to his satisfaction (with the exception of Brightlingsea). Of Moreton's failure to instigate a lifeboat launch by calling Mayday, Thomas pointed out that Moreton had alerted the rescue services at the first signs of trouble, had kept them informed, and had left the level of response up to them. He likened it to a patient describing his symptoms to a doctor, who would not expect to be denied treatment simply because he did not shout "Help!".

Russell Smith reiterated once more the seeming reluctance of the crew to help themselves. The dead could not reply.

No-one even dared to blame the Irish.

Apart from the special pleading, the enquiry had its simple moments, as when Mary Richards' account of her son's last evening at home was read, and when the recordings of the last messages on Channel 16 were played.

THE VENTILATOR PIPE, FILLER PIPE AND SOUNDING PIPE ON THE SISTER SHIP *UNION VENUS*. SEA WATER MUST HAVE ENTERED THE *UNION STAR'S* FUEL TANKS THROUGH ONE OF THESE PIPES.

The enquiry sat for 29 days between 14 March and 27 April 1983 at a cost of about £1.25 million.

Before its publication, those who cared about lifeboats had something more cheering to think about. The *Mabel Alice*, a spanking new 'Arun', had completed her sea trials and arrived on station at the beginning of May, cutting a great dash as she showed her paces around Mount's Bay. She was named in a special ceremony later in the summer by the Duke of Kent. A bottle of champagne, bought on his travels by Kevin Smith and saved for a special occasion, was donated by his mother to name her.

The enquiry report was published on 27 May. It found no one responsible, and blamed the weather.

Although there were cries of 'whitewash' it was not entirely toothless. It examined and rejected most of the criticisms of Moreton's actions. It merely stressed that reluctance to announce distress and over-optimism should be avoided by all careful seamen.

Moreton's main fault had probably been best expressed, in his idiosyncratic English, by Guy Buurman. "If the Union Star had given everybody a better impression about the situation which she was really in, then I think everybody would instead of walking be running, I do not know".

Of the coastguards the report concluded that with hindsight there was no question that the lifeboat should have been launched sooner. It recommended better liaison with the RNLI over specific terms, and less rigidity in interpretation of the general rules of when to recommend a launch. It did not blame any individual, though it did not fail to point out that "Others ... may have acted differently".

It recommended lengthening the three pipes on vessels like the Union Star, and, with a few other minor recommendations, passed into history. No one could say that the matter had not been thoroughly examined.

And there *was* the weather.

Each set of waves is different to a mariner, and each storm has its own signature. This one was characterised by its suddenness, violence, and power, which no meteorological records can fully show. The wind did not roar, it howled, and the waves did not pause when they hit the shore, but ran up the rocks as if they would never stop. It was the worst night and the worst place for an engine breakdown that ill fortune could have devised; and as for the lifeboat, the only wonder was not how she perished but how she survived as long as she did.

No one knows what happened in the few moments after the helicopter left and before the first helpers arrived. There were two left on the coaster and two in the sea wearing lifejackets. The lifeboat had already strayed far beyond the extremes of prudence. The consensus of opinion is that she did go back.

Although an autocratic coxswain, Trevelyan always consulted the crew at times of great risk. The language of heroism, except in fiction, is rarely heroic:

"What do you think boys?"

There would only be one answer. "Come on Trev, we can't leave them out here."

The bay below Boscawen must have been absolutely terrifying, even for experienced seamen, pitch dark, swept by vast breaking waves, with troughs down to the seaweed, boiling with foam, full of rocks and shoals. And yet time and again the tiny Watson pushed her bows into it, and achieved a rescue which ranks not only with the greatest in the history of the RNLI, but with any other human achievement. Finally, and for whatever reason, she lost the game of chance and was rolled onto the rocks; but the pride and gratitude her actions inspired could never be broken.

AFTERWORD

Time has passed. The families and friends of the lost crew keep their memories to themselves, in privacy and dignity. In Mousehole the Christmas lights still shine, though they are switched off for an hour every nineteenth of December. Tom Bawcock rides again. Damage has been done that will never mend but Mousehole, like most rural communities, is tough at the core, used to good times and bad.

After more than forty years public interest in the Penlee disaster has not slackened. Instead, with the help of the 2006 BBC documentary 'The Cruel Sea', it has entered the national consciousness as an example of the noblest instincts of human nature, an inspiration even to those who were not born at the time.

Visitors to West Cornwall may find several commemorations of the tragedy - the side chapel of St Clements Chapel, Mousehole dedicated to the lifeboatmen; the memorial stone and light in Paul Church; the memorial gardens beside the old Boathouse, now reduced by storms; the Boathouse itself, not open to the public but preserved exactly as it was left, still in working order; the plaque on the 'Ship' dedicated to Charlie Greenhaugh. However the best memorial of all can be found in Newlyn.

There at the pontoon sits the 'Severn' class lifeboat *Ivan Ellen*, a worthy successor to the *Mabel Alice* and all her predecessors, and next to her the fast-response inshore lifeboat *Mollie & Ivor Dent* which has saved so many who have fallen foul of Mount's Bay's changeable moods. Nigel Brockman's son Neil, spared on the night of the disaster, continued to volunteer and took over as Coxswain in 1992, leading the crew for a distinguished 17 years and earning the RNLI's Bronze Medal before handing over in turn to Patrick "Patch" Harvey, himself once saved by the Penlee Lifeboat. No memorial could please the men of the *Solomon Browne* more than to see the good work still going on, the 70-90 emergency missions carried out by Penlee every year, the same sense of purpose, the same selfless dedication.

Penlee lost a boat and a crew and even moved its location but a lifeboat station does not die. The determination that no-one at sea will ever be left to face danger alone drives the RNLI, the volunteer crews, the officers, the fund-raisers, the sponsors, those who leave legacies, the everyday donors, and all who make such a colossal task possible. The Penlee Lifeboat goes on, and the spirit of Trevelyan and his men will always sail with them.

If you see an RNLI collecting box, lend them a hand. They might be out again tonight...

LIFEBOAT IVAN ELLEN MOORED IN NEWLYN HARBOUR, 2012.